SOPHIA SWANN

Awaken As A Super Intuitive Empath, Develop Your Skills And Psychic
Empath Abilities And Protect Yourself Against Negative Energy,
Narcissists, & Energy Vampires

HEYOKA
&
DARK EMPATH
COLLECTION

Heyoka & Dark Empaths Collection

Awaken As A Super Intuitive Empath, Develop Your Skills And Psychic Empath Abilities And Protect Yourself Against Negative Energy, Narcissists, & Energy Vampires

Sophia Swann

DEVELOP YOUR UNMATCHED EMPATHIC & PSYCHIC ABILITIES
AND PROTECT THEM FROM NARCISSISTS & ENERGY VAMPIRES

HEYOKA
EMPATH AWAKENING

Embrace Your True Nature As The Most
Powerful Type Of Intuitive Empath

SOPHIA SWANN

Table of Contents

Introduction

Many things in life are far from cut and dried.

Science would like to tell you that everything has a theory, data to back it up, and metrics to prove and measure it. But there are many things about the world we live in that we can't explain.

The empath is one of them.

First things first, congratulations on downloading this book. You're about to go on a journey of discovery, and perhaps even self-discovery. Even if you don't think you're an empath, learning more about this magical and powerful phenomenon will change your life for the better. You'll become a more empathetic and sensitive person, and you'll learn how to avoid becoming overwhelmed in the process. Of course, if you are an empath, specifically a powerful Heyoka empath, there is much to learn, much to develop, and a lot to take on board!

First, We Need To Talk About You!

The fact you've downloaded this book tells us that you want to learn. You want to help others, and you want to look beyond science and rules, and dare to explore the unexplainable. By the end of this book, you'll be beyond all doubt that our minds and our energies are far more powerful than science would have you believe.

Most people don't want to change. That's a fact. But you do. Or at least, you want to become more knowledgeable and that's basically the same thing. The majority of people that buy books don't read them, in fact, it's thought that only 10% will actually read or listen to the book from start to finish. So, you're amongst the top 10% already! You're already standing out for all the right reasons.

Learning about the world of the Heyoka empath will change your outlook on life. It will show you that there is more about the world than you know right now. You might even realize that you **are** a Heyoka empath and in that case, the possibilities are endless. Let's be truthful - you picked up this book and that means that you already have an inkling that you could be an empath. Good for you!

Now you need to learn how to harness your gift for good. You need to understand how to manage it, protect yourself, and avoid becoming overwhelmed. When you do that, you can adopt a positive mindset and use it to help others and to help yourself too.

Change occurs right now. The moment you turn the first page.

Why Is Everyone So Fascinated by Empaths?

In all honesty, we're fascinated by empaths because we don't understand them. It's not something we can prove. It's only something you can feel if you are an empath.

The ability to take on someone else's emotions as your own can be terrifying if you don't know what's happening or why. But consider the positives for a second. It's a gift. You can help someone handle a problem. You can give advice. You're the only person who feels what they feel. It's a blessing and something you need to harness and use every day.

But, we're fascinated because so many people like to push the idea away and dismiss it as nothing but hocus pocus. How do you explain mediumship? How do you explain intuition? How do you explain predictions? These are all things connected with empaths and let's be truthful, it's hard to dismiss them all as hocus pocus.

By the end of this book, your fascination will be at another level. You'll be knowledgeable and you'll be able to open your mind to the boundless energies that are around us all right this second. Not only that, but you'll want to learn about your own gifts. It may be that you truly are a born Heyoka. You have so much power and capability inside of you, and it's just sitting there, waiting to be awoken and unleashed on the world for the greater good.

It's beyond fascinating, it's captivating!

So, let's not waste another second. It's time to lift the lid on the world of the empath and learn more about the most powerful and sacred of them all - the Heyoka empath.

What you learn will change your mind set for life.

Ready?

Then let's dive in…

Chapter 1:
An Introduction to The Fascinating World of Empaths

You've made it to the first chapter! That means you're keen to learn more about the world of the Heyoka empath and about empaths overall. You're about to embark on a journey that will change the way you look at the world forever.

Empaths are real. Some call them 'earth angels', but their guiding and shining light is something that has the power not only to take a bad day and make it good, but it can also change the entire direction of a person's life.

What you believe about empaths now is probably only the very tip of the iceberg. You're about to learn so much more.

Whether you consider yourself to be an empath, or you think might be, learning about the whole subject is a good idea. Even if you're not an empath, perhaps you're someone who is simply highly sensitive. While that means something a little different from being an actual empath, much of the advice on how to handle the situation still applies.

In this chapter, we're going to introduce the idea of an empath to you. We're not going to get into the specifics of the Heyoka empath just yet. Before we get there, you need to know what an empath actually is, why it's different from simply being sensitive, and the different types of empaths. Then, we can move on to the specifics and help you to harness your gift and manage it in a way that helps you feel more confident and comfortable.

So, are you ready to get started on your empath journey?

Hold on tight!

What Is The Difference Between Being an Empath and Being a Highly Sensitive Person?

First things first, before we get into the magical stuff, we need to give a few definitions.

The words 'empath' and 'empathy' are often confused. Then, we throw 'highly sensitive' into the mix. They're all different but can often be used interchangeably - totally incorrectly!

If you want to learn about the world of a Heyoka empath, in fact, the world of any empath, then you need to know exactly what one is and why simply being sensitive or empathetic isn't the same thing.

Let's start with empathy.

Most people have empathy. The only people who don't have much or any empathy are thought to be narcissists. When you have empathy, you're able to walk a mile in someone's shoes and understand how they feel. That affects how you communicate with them and how you act around them.

For instance, if someone is feeling down because they've lost their job, you're able to understand that they're worried about where their next paycheck is going to come from. You know that because you're able to imagine yourself in that situation and how you would feel. As such, you'll be kind to them and lend them a listening ear.

Empathy comes from our kindness but also from our life experiences. If you've been heartbroken before, you'll be able to show empathy to someone who is currently going through a breakup because you know how it feels to be in the same situation. You can appreciate that we all feel things differently, but you know that it's a terrible feeling and you can sympathize with them all the same.

So, how is that different from being an empath?

While an empath has empathy, in fact, they have a lot, they don't just understand how someone feels. They actually feel it.

For instance, if an empath is standing next to someone at the bus stop and that person is feeling angry because they've had an argument with their boss, the empath might suddenly start feeling angry for no specific reason. They may not even know this person or have any clue that they had a bad day at work.

Put simply, an empath takes on the emotions of those around them and feels them as if they were their own. But, they know that those emotions don't belong to them because they've no reason to feel that way. They soak up emotions like a sponge and it can be extremely overwhelming if they don't understand how to handle it.

For instance, an empath may find that standing in a room full of people is extremely overwhelming. They may feel a million different emotions all at one time and that's because they're absorbing the energies from the people around them. Many empaths simply don't like to spend time in large groups and much prefer to be alone or in small groups of people whom they trust. They also find a lot of peace and solitude in nature.

So, we have two terms defined. Empathy is something most of us have, when we're able to understand how someone feels by putting ourselves in their shoes. Being an empath means that you literally feel those emotions as your own, even when you have no idea what is wrong with that person.

Let's introduce another term - highly sensitive person, or HSP.

It's very easy to confuse an empath and an HSP. But, they are subtly different.

A highly sensitive person is normally an introvert, but an empath can be introverted or extroverted. An HSP shares many traits with an empath. For instance, they're very sensitive to light and noise, they're extremely empathetic, and they become overwhelmed when spending time in large groups or busy environments. They also need regular time alone to recharge and destress. But, an HSP doesn't absorb emotions in the same way as an empath.

They are often able to pick up on something, i.e. the idea that someone isn't feeling their best, but they can't pinpoint what the emotion is because they're not taking it on as their own. Despite that, HSPs can help others because they can tell that something is wrong and then they can try to get them to open up.

When you live your life as an HSP or an empath, it's easy for things to become a little too much. It's vital that you learn how to handle your personality and your gift. While it's true that HSPs aren't empaths, a lot of the advice we're going to give throughout this book on how to handle extreme emotions will still work for you. So, if you don't identify as an actual empath, still take on what we say and try it in your own daily life.

But, if you do believe you're an empath, the next step is to identify what type of empath you are. By doing this you'll be able to pinpoint your specific triggers and tailor your management plan accordingly. Of course, the rest of this book is going to talk specifically about the Heyoka empath. You'll soon come to realize that the Heyoka empath is one of the most powerful on the planet. This is someone with amazing potential to help others, but that comes at a cost - absorption of countless emotions that don't belong to you.

The Different Types of Empaths

In our next chapter, we're going to talk at length about the Heyoka empath, but what other types of empath are there?

There are thought to be 11 different types of an empath and that might lead you to think that a huge amount of people are walking around with empathic gifts they don't know about. The truth is that a true empath is quite rare. It's thought that only around 1-2% of the world's population are true empaths, but millions are HSPs, or perhaps even borderline empaths.

Let's talk about the 11 different types of an empath and then we can focus ourselves completely upon the most powerful of them all - the Heyoka empath.

The Intuitive Empath or Claircognizant Empath

This type of empath uses their intuition heavily and they have an ability to just "know" how to handle a situation. They may not have any experience of the situation, but their ability tells them exactly what to do or say to make things better.

In terms of reacting to other people, a claircognizant empath can read another person like a book and understand exactly what they're feeling by spending just a few seconds in their company.

The Telepathic Empath

A little like a mind-reader, a telepathic empath can read a person's feelings or thoughts by spending a few seconds with them. The person doesn't need to say anything, but the empath picks up on their energies automatically. This type of empath is also a little akin to the psychometric empath, as some are able to use objects in the same way.

The Precognitive Empath

This type of empath is able to predict events before they occur. This is normally through a dream and is often connected to the empath feeling a huge amount of anxiety, or a feeling they can't pinpoint - it's almost a feeling that "something isn't quite right". Then, when exploring the feeling further, they can understand the event that is yet to occur, via their strong intuition.

The Psychometric Empath

A person who identifies as a psychometric empath can use objects to understand how a person is feeling or what is going on with them. For instance, they can touch a necklace belonging to that person and they will understand more about them. They can also use photographs to get the same type of information.

The Physical Empath

You might hear the physical empath also called the 'medical empath'. This is someone who is able to feel another person's pain as their own. For instance, if someone has a stomachache, the empath will start to feel like they have a stomach ache too.

In this case, the physical empath is able to warn someone when they feel like they should go to the doctor and get something checked out.

The Emotional Empath

The emotional empath is probably the classical type of empath that we all think of when we hear the term. This is someone who is able to pick up on the emotions of others because they absorb them as their own. They're able to understand how a person is feeling without words having to be spoken and as a result, they can work out what is happening to make them feel that way.

The Flora Empath

This is a rare type of empath but they are able to communicate with plants and read their energies. This type of empath is extremely in touch with nature and they're able to understand what the plant needs, e.g., water, food, sunlight. It is also thought that if a plant is sick, a flora empath is able to help them heal.

The Geomantic Empath

Continuing with the nature theme, a geomantic empath is able to understand the earth, particularly the soil. This type of empath may be able to predict natural disasters by reading signs in the lead-up to the event. For instance, a geomantic empath may be able to read signs that a hurricane is on the way, or maybe even an earthquake, due to changes in the energy around them.

The Psychic Empath/Medium

We're all quite familiar with the word 'medium' but many don't realize that it's actually a type of empath too - a psychic empath. This type of empath is able to communicate with spirits that have passed. Some can sense them, some can hear them, and some can feel them.

The Fauna Empath/Animal Empaths

If flora empaths can communicate with plants, fauna, or animal empaths have the ability to communicate and understand animals on a deeper level. They're able to send psychic messages by touch although it is thought that animals don't reach out to fauna empaths directly, and it's normally the empath who initiates contact first.

13

The Heyoka Empath

And now onto the main subject of our book! We're going to talk in great depth about the Heyoka empath, the most powerful of all empaths. This type of empath has a great amount of potential to help others but is also quite misunderstood. Life as a Heyoka empath can be challenging at times, but by learning how to harness your power and manage your gift, you'll not only be able to help others, but you'll be able to help yourself too.

These are the main 11 types of empath but as we're learning more and more about this subject as time goes on, it's entirely possible that we will discover other types in the future.

Do you identify with any of the short descriptions above? If so, pursue your line of inquiry more. Learning how to harness the power of your gift is important and by doing that, you're able to learn how to avoid becoming overwhelmed in the process.

You Have a Gift!

Before we move on to talking solely about the Heyoka empath, we need to mention one thing. If you're an empath, whatever type, understand that you have a gift.

For sure, it may not seem that way when you're overwhelmed and struggling with emotions flying at you from all directions, but there is a silver lining to all of this.

You can learn to manage your gift and harness it for good. You can learn how to sidestep the negative points and understand when you need time alone, to regroup. Your gift allows you to help other people because you understand them on a level that nobody else does. You actually feel what they feel - the only other person besides them. So, you can give them advice, should they want it, and you can offer them help and a little kindness to cheer them up and make their day a little easier.

Depending upon which type of empath you identify as will determine how you feel the energies and emotions around you and what you can do about them. For instance, if you're a medical empath, feeling something that another person is physically feeling may be quite distressing at first. But as you learn how to handle your gift, you'll see that you can perhaps encourage that person to seek help and treatment. Who knows, you may actually save a life.

Being an empath is nothing short of a gift, but the truth is that most empaths simply don't understand how to harness the power of their gift and manage it in a way that doesn't cause them to feel completely overwhelmed most of the time. The good news is that you can tick all of those boxes and learn how to enjoy being an empath.

While we're going to talk specifically about the Heyoka empath, know that a lot of the advice on how to handle being an empath will work for you, no matter what type you identify as.

Points to Remember

How do you feel about the world of the empath? Intrigued? Keen to learn more? That's the spirit!

Learning about the empathic gift is really quite special. While true empaths are rare, many people on the planet have some traits of an empath and that can, in many cases, allow them to develop into empaths themselves.

In this chapter, we've talked generally about empaths. We know that empathy and the empath are two different things, and we know that highly sensitive people, or HSPs, are a little different from empaths too. We've also talked about the 11 types of empath we know about so far.

The main takeaway from this chapter is that while life as an empath may be difficult when unmanaged, it's a true gift. You can learn how to manage your life as an empath and from there, only magical things will happen!

So, are you ready to learn about the most powerful empath of them all?

Let's introduce the world of the Heyoka empath.

Chapter 2:
What Does It Means To Be A Heyoka Empath

Can you imagine having the power to help other people heal? Can you imagine how it feels to know that you had a major hand in improving someone's life? That's what a Heyoka empath can do.

We know there are different types of an empath, and perhaps even more that are yet to be discovered. But, we are certain about the fact that the Heyoka empath is an empath like no other.

In this chapter, we're going to talk about what a Heyoka empath is and what makes them so special. Why is this particular type of empath so powerful? What is it about this type of empath that gives them the ability to heal and change lives?

All is about to be revealed!

The Heyoka Is The Most Powerful Empath

First, let's explain what the Heyoka empath is and where the name came from.

The Heyoka empath is pronounced hey-oh-kah, and it's considered to be the most powerful of them all. The name is derived from the language of the Lakota people, a Native American tribe, which means 'sacred clown', or 'fool'.

Now, it's easy to read that definition and think that there is nothing powerful about being a fool. But, wait for a second, there's far more to it.

The word relates to the fact that the Heyoka empath is able to use humor for healing. They use their keen sense of humor to encourage people to think outside of the box, to explore their behavior and new ideas, and to open their minds to new perspectives and ways of thinking. All of this is done without explanation or reason, it simply happens. It's the gift of the Heyoka empath, and it's even possible that the empaths themselves don't realize what they're doing at that very moment.

The type of humor that a Heyoka empath uses is quite dark and satirical. They make fun of things to make them seem less serious and to allow people to explore new solutions and ways forward. When you look at a situation without humor, in the cold light of day, it's easy to take it too seriously. You can't see the woods for the trees because everything seems so bleak. However, when you add humor to the situation, you realize that it can't be as bad as you thought. If you're able to laugh at it then maybe there is a way around it. That's what the Heyoka empath does.

The humor isn't designed to poke fun at people, only situations. By doing that, the person is encouraged to look for ways to handle the problem and heal from it. Otherwise, they would have been stuck, wallowing, moving in neither direction.

You might read this and assume that Heyoka empaths are detached and lighthearted by the fact they use humor. But that's not the truth. They use humor as a mechanism, but at the end of the day, they're still regular empaths. They still absorb the feelings of others very easily and can become overwhelmed without understanding how to manage their gift.

Heyoka empaths are extremely sensitive and that's what stops them from using humor to make fun of people. They're unable to do so because of their empathy and sensitivities. They want to help, they don't want to poke fun at people. Their sole focus is on helping others.

In fact, the main function of a Heyoka empath is to act as a teacher and a mirror. When they absorb the emotions of others and understand that someone is dealing with negativity and pain, they reflect that situation back to them via their role as a 'mirror'. Then, they poke fun at the situation to drag the person out of their negative funk. They force them (gently) to see a different way, to see a different perspective.

As such, the Heyoka acts as a teacher because they open up a world of self-discovery and exploration. The person who is struggling can then carefully examine the situation they are in, seeing it as less of a negative and more of a growth opportunity. Their behavior and problems are reflected back to them by the 'mirror' and as such, they're able to examine areas for change.

Understanding something you can't feel is indeed hard but think for a second. Do you often use humor to help others? Do you find joy in taking someone in a bad mood and turning their mood into a smile? Do you enjoy seeing that lightbulb moment of "oh wait for a second, maybe this isn't so bad" flash in their eyes?

If so, you might be a Heyoka empath.

How is the Heyoka Empath Different From Other Empaths?

All empaths are highly sensitive and have a large degree of empathy. In fact, on the empathy scale, you have empaths at the extreme end and narcissists at the zero end. Everyone else falls at some point along the rest of the scale, with highly sensitive people (HSPs) further towards the end where empaths sit.

Whether a psychic empath, a flora empath, or a medical empath, every type of empath has the ability to read subtle energies around them. A Heyoka empath has every one of the 'regular' empath abilities, but they take this up a notch or two. Their ability to use humor is the way in which they connect with others and act in the role of a teacher.

In our last section, we mentioned that the Heyoka empath acts as a mirror. They reflect the situation or emotion back to the person dealing with it and then use satirical humor to get them to see that it's not that bad and that there is a way around it. From there, the role of the teacher begins.

That's what makes the Heyoka empath the most powerful.

It isn't just a case of absorbing a feeling and knowing how someone feels. Although that's always extremely valuable because it allows you to connect with that person. It's more than that for the Heyoka empath. In this case, they're acting as a guide. They're showing the person a different way, and from there, they're able to assist them in exploring the situation and how it could be solved. It's almost like the Heyoka empath is acting as a mirror to the person's strengths and weaknesses, showing them a movie almost in real-time of how things could be different.

In truth, humor is extremely powerful. Dragging someone out of negativity is never easy but that is the unique gift of the Heyoka empath.

The role of the Heyoka is disruption, but in the most positive of ways. Just like the 'fool' or 'clown', they're named after, they're designed to mess things up a little, shake up the order. When the empath reflects a person's problems or behavior back to them, they're likely to know exactly what to say to make them think 'oh, wait a minute'. This changes the energy in the room and moves things from negative to positive.

Does the Heyoka empath heal gently and calmly? No. They do quite the opposite.

The truth is that when someone becomes aware of a problem, or a problematic element of their behavior, it can be upsetting. But, awareness leads to healing. This situation can help someone move on from a situation that isn't meant for them or one that is simply not serving them well anymore. By reflecting that behavior or problem back to them, they can see what's going on, and the humor elements help them to look for different routes forward.

It's not calm, it's not gentle, and it can be quite chaotic, but it does exactly what it's meant to do - the approach helps the person to heal.

The Heyoka Doesn't Follow the Crowd

The most striking thing about a Heyoka empath, aside from their remarkable ability to heal, is that they're simply not like anyone else. They're individual in every single way it is possible to be.

A Heyoka empath usually feels quite self-assured. They don't have an interest in following the crowd and they usually feel like they simply don't fit in. As such, they learn to become happy with their own company and follow their own path, rather than anyone else's.

However, this is only the case for a Heyoka empath who has learned to handle and manage their gift. It's very easy for an empath's life to spiral out of control when they aren't aware of their empathic nature, and that's often ten times stronger for an unaware Heyoka empath. Knowing themselves comes down to understanding their gift. That's not always the easiest process, thanks to the world's general distrust of anything that cannot be seen or measured. Indeed, an empath's ability can only really be felt by the empath and passed around by stories of how they helped.

In this type of situation, people like to push their hunches aside and put it down to nothing but coincidence. Can you imagine how many

Heyoka empaths are walking around unaware of their amazing gifts and how to manage them and not feel totally overwhelmed every single day of their lives?

Points to Remember

In this chapter, we've introduced the most powerful of all empath types - the Heyoka empath. The name is derived from the Lakota language, meaning 'sacred clown', or 'fool', yet there is nothing foolish about this type of empath.

While all empaths have the power to help people, the Heyoka empath has the power to heel. They act as a mirror, reflecting traits and behaviors back at people so they can recognize patterns and make changes. This is done by using humor to suck out negativity and install a sense of positivity, with new possibilities all around.

The humor a Heyoka empath uses is never to hurt or upset anyone. It may be satirical at times, but it's never aimed at that particular person, only to make light of the situation. While how a Heyoka empath heals may not be calm or tranquil, it does exactly what needs to be done - it helps people to move away from situations that aren't serving them well in life. From there, that person can look toward new avenues and make great changes in their lives.

The Heyoka empath isn't someone who follows the crowd, and they likely feel they somehow don't quite fit in. But, that's what makes them so wonderful!

Of course, when an empath doesn't realize their empathic ways, life can be difficult. That's why a Heyoka empath in particular needs to understand their power and potential, learn to manage it, and understand when they may be feeling overwhelmed. In the coming chapters, we're going to talk in much more detail about how to recognize whether you're a Heyoka empath and what to do to manage your gift and use it for the greater good of you and everyone around you.

Chapter 3:
Signs & Traits of The Heyoka

We know what you're thinking - you're dying to know whether you might be a Heyoka empath! You've learned about what this type of empath can do and now you're keen to know more. You want to understand the traits, the benefits, the disadvantages, and the signs that lead a person to think "ah-ha, that's me!"

Well, you're in luck. In this chapter, we're going to delve further into the world of the Heyoka empath and understand far more about what makes this powerful type of empath tick. By the end, you'll have a much stronger feeling about whether you're a Heyoka empath or whether you might be a different type entirely.

Traits of a Heyoka

Signs and traits are different things. If you want to know if you're perhaps a Heyoka empath, you'll need to think very carefully and examine many different avenues. First, we need to think about personality traits and then we need to consider solid signs and evidence. So, let's talk about personality traits first of all.

A Heyoka empath, as we know, shares the same empathic gifts as other empaths, but they take everything to a much higher level. They're always aware of the energies around them and the peaks and troughs when they meet someone who is struggling with negativity. It's almost like a radar going off in their head that guides them towards a person who needs their help.

A Heyoka empath will likely be drawn towards creative career paths, such as design, writing, or artistic means. They're also likely to be introverted, although that's not always the case for everyone. A constant battle between light energy and dark energy, Heyoka

24

empaths have many conflicting traits that often lead them to feel like they don't quite fit in.

Let's explore some of the most common traits of a Heyoka empath.

You Have a Strong Intuition

All empaths have highly developed intuitive skills, but a Heyoka empath's intuition is off the scale. You'll probably notice that your gut feeling is extremely strong at times, and it tries to lead you towards people or situations that need your help. You tend to understand what's going on without knowing anything about the situation at all. You are also very talented at understanding when someone isn't quite telling the truth.

You're a Creative Person

Most Heyoka empaths are quite creative and, as before, usually go down career paths that allow them to use these skills. Even if you don't use your creativity in your working life, you'll probably spend a lot of your downtime indulging in a creative hobby, such as painting, writing, or making things with your hands.

You Enjoy Solving Puzzles

Most Heyokas find solving puzzles quite soothing. While you're very intuitive, you're also logical at times. You like to get to the bottom of things and solve the problem. Because of your mirror tendencies when healing others, you find that you're able to look at problems from your outer standpoint and then examine them from an emotional view too. This gives you a great advantage when solving an issue.

You Can Feel the Emotions of Others

As an empath, you can notice and soak up the emotions of those around you, taking them on as your own. Again, this can be very overwhelming if you don't learn how to protect yourself and take time out. It's also likely that you can automatically tell if someone isn't telling you the truth. You read the energies of those around you and you're rarely wrong about how they're feeling.

You Struggle to Control Your Emotions

Some Heyoka empaths struggle with bipolar tendencies, but not all. Yet even those who don't will probably find that their emotions can often swing wildly. The fact that you're able to soak up the extreme emotions of others, usually negative, can lead you towards angry or emotional outbursts. Being able to handle your gift is important if you want to avoid feeling totally overwhelmed much of the time.

You're Introverted

This isn't always the case, but most Heyoka empaths are introverted. You're often juggling many different thoughts and emotions at any one time, which leads you to be quite quiet and often 'in your own head'. People may struggle to talk to you sometimes, because you're often daydreaming or lost in your own thoughts.

You Read Body Language Very Easily

You can read people very well and that means you're able to pick up on the slightest change in someone's body language or their tone of voice. You don't necessarily listen to what people are saying, because you know that people can lie. Instead, you read their non-verbal cues and put the puzzle together to give you the correct picture.

You're Often Late

Your time management skills leave a lot to be desired and you're often late or struggle with handing things in on time. You find balancing a lot of things at once quite overwhelming, simply because you're dealing with the emotions that are flying around all at once. You may find that you're often late or that you forget things.

Your Senses Are Highly Developed

Your general senses are very sensitive and you're able to see things that other people cannot. You're also very good at noticing patterns in things and reading situations that you don't really know a lot about, to begin with.

You're a Bit of a Perfectionist

Heyoka empaths are a little different from other empaths, in that their energy is both light and dark. This is because of the amount of negativity they encounter in their lives. This can often cause them to be too hard on themselves and they're prone to developing perfectionist tendencies.

You Don't Handle Criticism Well

Most people don't enjoy being told when they haven't done something to the best of their ability or that what they've done isn't the best. But, a Heyoka empath really doesn't like it! This is particularly the case with any criticism of their creative work.

All empaths are sensitive, but the Heyoka is even more so, especially in this regard. They will take any criticism, no matter how well-meaning, totally to heart.

You're Indecisive

Heyokas can help other people very easily, but they often struggle with making their own decisions. They can use their intuition as a guide but when it comes to making that final choice, they often doubt themselves and lack confidence in their ability to get it right. But, you're also extremely open-minded which is perhaps another reason why decisions are hard for you - you can see so many options in front of you.

The Heyoka empath is different. They're not like anyone else. That means there are possible traits that you also have that set you apart from the so-called majority. For instance, it's thought that Heyoka empaths (some, not all) have a higher chance of being left-handed. Again, the majority of people are right-handed, so it makes sense.

It's also thought that Heyoka empaths have a greater chance of:

- Being dyslexic
- Looking younger for their actual age
- Having been born in the breech position

But, that doesn't mean that you have to tick one of the three points above to be a Heyoka. These are simply more likely, yet not certainties.

Overall, how many of these personality traits do you recognize? It's important to remember that just because these are common traits of a Heyoka empath, it doesn't mean that you're going to be able to tick every single one off the list. Everyone is different and it could be that you're a blend of two different empath types, or that you're simply not going to fit into the so-called mold.

That's a good sign of a Heyoka in itself. This type of empath just doesn't fit in. They often feel like they stand out and don't tend to follow the same patterns as everyone else. They tend to follow different paths to other people and this likely happened during adolescence and they don't quite understand it. Of course, that could lead to a huge amount of upset because all teenagers want to fit in with their peers.

The point of this chapter is to help you identify whether or not you're a Heyoka empath. If you're not, simply learning about this powerful and intriguing type of empath is extremely interesting. But, by knowing if you're a Heyoka, you'll gain even more benefit from our later chapters, when we go on to talk about how to handle your gift.

Life as a Heyoka isn't easy. But, it can be rewarding if you know how to avoid taking on too much darkness.

13 Powerful Signs That You Are a Heyoka Empath

We've talked about personality traits, but signs are a completely different thing. These are the pointers that give you a strong indication that a Heyoka way of life could be your calling. It's easy to ignore signs. It's easy to miss them if you're not sure what's going on. But, by bringing awareness to the situation, it's possible to face up to your abilities as an empath and learn how to handle them suitably.

Let's look at the main signs of a Heyoka empath situation.

You Are Drawn Towards Negativity

A Heyoka empath picks up on the energies and emotions around them. This has a flip side and a downside. There are positive energies everywhere and you do notice them, but because of your ability to act as a mirror and teacher to those you're supposed to heal, you find that you're most commonly drawn to negative situations instead.

If you find that you're often picking up on the anger, upset, depression, and general negativity of people around you, that could be for a reason. You're meant to help these people. Of course, that can be difficult to deal with because being around negativity much of the time will drag you down.

You're Able to Observe Life Without Reacting

This particular sign may not be something you can nod along to right now. But, as you learn to manage your Heyoka gift, it will come to you. Some Heyoka empaths are able to just roll with the punches from the start, but others need to understand what is going on and learn to manage their gift first.

Either way, a Heyoka empath has a high amount of emotional intelligence. That means they're able to observe life from the outside and work it out, without having to react instantly. Again, this is something that will come to you with practice if it hasn't already.

This particular sign is thought to be down to the fact that Heyoka empaths are very wise. They know how to handle people and situations and they know that there is always a way out of any problem.

People Come to You for Advice

Do you find the people tend to be drawn towards you for advice and deep conversation? Do you actually enjoy giving advice to other people? If so, there's a chance that you're a Heyoka empath, as long as you can agree with several other signs on the list.

Your sole purpose is to help others by reflecting back on them (via the mirror) and using humor to help them see another way. People are drawn to you because humor is disarming but also because they can sense that you're different.

It's almost instinctive. You simply feel that you need to help someone and, what's more, you really want to do so. Once you've done what you need to do, you feel a sense of pride, but you may also feel tired because you've expended a huge amount of energy during the process.

You Hate Lies and Can Sense a Liar a Mile Away

Your intuition is very strong, and you can read body language and non-verbal cues very well. That's something we've already covered in our traits section. But, do you get an overwhelming sense that someone is lying occasionally? Is that feeling so strong that you just know, you can tell 100% that they're not telling the truth?

Heyoka empaths do not like lies, even small, white lies. They appreciate truth and total honesty and their ability to know when someone isn't being truthful is extremely strong.

This is one of the perks of being a Heyoka because you're never in doubt that someone isn't being truthful to you. As such, you're very unlikely to be taken advantage of in that way.

You Tend to Know What Someone is Going to Say

Heyoka empaths are very powerful and that means that in some way, they're a mishmash of other empath types too. While a Heyoka isn't necessarily going to be able to read people's minds, they can read people very deeply and as such, you may find that as a Heyoka, you'll know what someone is going to say. You might also notice that you finish their sentences for them. After all, you're feeling what they're feeling so you're literally in their head anyway.

You Feel Recharged and Lighter When You've Spent Time Alone

Do you often feel totally overwhelmed when you've spent time around people? When you're in a group of people, do you feel like you have to get away otherwise your head is going to explode? That's because you're absorbing energies and emotions from all the people around you and you can only take so much on board.

It's very likely that you'll feel recharged and much lighter on your feet when you've spent some time alone. This is probably doubly the case if you've spent time in nature, e.g. in the mountains, the beach, in a field, or even sitting in your garden.

You Evoke Strong Reactions in Those Around You

You affect people in ways that nobody else can. It's almost like you rub them up the wrong way or really get under their skin. You cause them to feel overly emotional and make them think of situations that they perhaps don't want to address. This is you acting as a mirror to them and making them think of their behavior and situations. Of course, that also means that you soak up those emotions, which can be difficult for you.

Many Heyoka empaths find it hard to have relationships because of this very fact. They affect people so strongly that their relationships are often over before they begin. But, it's not impossible - that's something we'll explore more in a later chapter.

You Find Humor Comes Easily to You

Of course, the main purpose of a Heyoka empath is to use humor to help people heal. So, it's very likely, in fact, it's extremely likely, that you have a fantastic sense of humor, and those witty one-liners everyone dreams of getting at the right time, just come to you whenever you need them. You're able to make things lighter and help people to feel better, even when you're surrounded by negativity.

It's possible that you've always been considered the 'funny one' in your friend group or when you were at school. That's for a reason - your Heyoka ways depend upon it.

You're Able to Come up With Creative Solutions to Problems

We mentioned in the traits section that Heyoka empaths are natural problem solvers, but the difference between you and someone who's simply good at coming up with answers is that you tend to think totally creatively. You think in ways that nobody else does and you're completely 'out of the box' with your suggestions. Some of these work wonderfully well, but others aren't well-received because they seem so left-field.

You enjoy coming up with these conclusions and you find sometimes that your mind runs away with you and you're coming up with all manner of solutions so fast that you can't keep track of them.

You Often Know What to Say to Make Someone Feel Better

Empaths in general tend to have a knack for saying the right thing, at the right time. You have that doubly because of your use of humor. If you find that you're able to make people feel better with a few words, or that you rarely seem to 'put your foot in it' and say the wrong thing, it's probably down to your empathic ways.

However, you're not someone who lies about anything when making someone feel better. Remember, Heyoka empaths do not like liars and that means you're not going to say anything untrue, in any situation, either.

You Struggle with Sleep

Do you find that you often struggle to get a good night's sleep? Or, do you have insomnia in general? It's very common for empaths to struggle with sleep and that's because of a need to off-load and disconnect from the countless emotions they've soaked up throughout the day. However, with the powerful gift of an empath comes an even deeper need to get a good night's sleep, and that's not always easy to come by.

People Are Sometimes Unsure of How to Act Around You

You may find that people act strangely around you at first. Again, people don't like to be faced with troublesome behavior or problems and you're mirroring that back to them. They're not sure how or why, and they can't quite put their finger on what's going on, but they feel unsure of you. That's one of the key signs that you're a Heyoka empath.

The most important thing in this situation is not to feel upset by the reactions of those around you. You're trying to help and sometimes it takes a little time for people to feel comfortable and understand that despite your unorthodox approach (something they don't understand), you're actually showing them a new way forward.

You may not be able to nod along to every single one of these signs right now. It could be that you've not realized or embraced your empathic nature yet, or that a particular sign simply doesn't apply to you. We're all different and all Heyoka empaths are slightly different too. But it's very likely that you can nod along to at least half, or possibly most signs.

In that case, it's time to explore your Heyoka nature a little more. In the coming chapters, we're going to talk about how to manage your gift. But, even if you're not Heyoka, much of the advice we're going to give will help you in your general life too. Learning to focus on yourself and destress is important for everyone - empath or not.

You Don't Feel the Need to Fit in

Most people want to fit in, to blend in even. Not you. As a Heyoka empath, you've always been different and as you grow, you learn that it doesn't matter whether you fit in or not. You love to go against the norm, and you don't feel the need to be accepted by society anymore. That's a sure sign that you've grown into your power and accepted your Heyoka gift.

It's also possible that the way in which you help people heal is also a reason for your lack of fitting in. You tend to say things that are shocking. Remember, Heyokas don't heal calmly, they shake things up. While that's never done offensively, it may be something that causes people to stop, pinch their eyebrows together and feel a little 'put out' for a second. None of this helps anyone to fit in, not least someone who makes others face problems they perhaps don't want to face, to begin with. Remember, you're painfully honest sometimes and not everyone appreciates that.

Healing Others With Humor

As a Heyoka, you can pick up energy in the air and make quick sense of it. But, how do you use humor to help others and allow them to start healing?

Heyokas have different tactics for this, which they often use subconsciously, without thinking about it. However, they also mirror the behavior of the other person so they can reflect back and show them how the problem looks from the outside. That's when humor steps in.

So, how do Heyoka empaths use humor to get people to start healing from problems and situations? Here are a few ways.

To Help People Open Up

We've mentioned before that humor is quite disarming. When someone uses gentle humor, you tend to feel like you can open up and trust them. This is something Heyokas do very well. We've already mentioned that people tend to feel unsure of how to react to Heyokas at first, but this tactic is a great way to win people around and get them to feel more comfortable in your presence.

To Allow the Absorption of Healing Energy

Again, this is about relaxation. When a person is thinking more positively and has relaxed enough to open up to the empath, the energy shifts. They're more open to absorbing healing energies and more likely to notice the reflection that the empath is mirroring back to them.

To Change Their Perspective Away from Negativity

Again, humor helps people to relax but it can also be very useful in sucking negativity right out of any situation. When you can laugh at something, it doesn't seem quite so bad, right? That's exactly what this tactic does. Then, the person is able to think more positively, and that allows them to open up to new solutions.

Nobody can think of how to change a situation, or even want to change a situation when they're stuck in a negative thought pattern. By using humor, the Heyoka can get the person to relax, think more positively, and then they can start to explore solutions.

Shocking or Nudging People Out of Rigid Mindsets

Heyokas often use satirical humor, and this is very useful for shocking someone out of a mindset that could be considered rigid or restrictive. When someone refuses to see other avenues out of a problem, they're never going to escape its clutches. However, if a

Heyoka can shock them out of it, using a well-timed piece of humor designed to make them question their line of thinking, they're able to change their perspective and see new routes forward.

This can often be a watershed moment because they suddenly feel uplifted and positive. They realize that they've been stuck in a situation needlessly.

Talking in Riddles

The idea of helping someone to heal isn't about telling them what they need to do. In this case, the empath isn't getting a message from spirit, they're not a medium or a clairvoyant. Instead, they're encouraging the person with the issue to start examining different possibilities. To that aim, the empath doesn't give instructions, they talk in riddles and answer questions with new questions. The idea is to get the person to examine things themselves, not give them the answers.

Can you see how powerful humor can be? It's almost like a Heyoka empath is an all-knowing entity! Their ability to pick up on heavy energies in their sphere helps them to zero in on the people who need their help the most. By using humor, they're able to get people to trust them and they can start to unpick the layers of negativity that person has probably built up over time.

Then comes the moment the healing begins.

Points to Remember

This chapter has been a pretty long one because we've talked at length about how you can recognize whether or not you're a Heyoka empath yourself. Maybe you are, maybe you're not, but either way, it's an interesting topic!

Heyoka empaths are special on many levels, but they often feel like they don't fit in. This can be upsetting if they haven't yet understood their empath nature. However, they also somehow know that they're supposed to do good work and as they grow into themselves, they understand their gift.

It's not always the case that you'll be able to nod along to every single trait and sign. Maybe you can only identify with half. But that's a good start. From there, you can open yourself up to recognizing the energies around you and developing your gift.

Of course, the next step is learning how to manage being a Heyoka empath and not allowing it to cause you discomfort or upset. That's what we're going to move on to shortly. For now, the main points to remember from this chapter are the signs and traits of a Heyoka and how they use humor to help people start healing from problems and situations they've found themselves in.

When you dig into how the Heyoka empath works, it's really quite captivating, isn't it?

Chapter 4:
Life as a Heyoka

You might wonder whether a person who is born a Heyoka empath is able to embrace their gift and understand it. That's the hard part.

For many empaths of this nature, they don't understand their gift until at least their 20s onwards. For some, it can be much later. The awareness of what an empath is may not come to them and they struggle with not being able to understand how they have such a strong effect on people. It's also very easy to become overwhelmed and simply feel negative a lot of the time.

In this chapter, we're going to shine a light on the day-to-day life of a Heyoka empath. For sure, the experience will be different from person to person, but we can generalize to a large degree. From there, we can move on to giving advice and help on how to make your life as this powerful type of empath much easier and extremely rewarding.

It's very easy to focus upon the negative aspects of life as Heyoka. And, we can't ignore the fact that there are some downsides. However, the main shining light in all of this is your ability to heal in a way that nobody else can.

By focusing upon that very strong positive, you can overcome anything else that life throws at you.

Being a Heyoka Empath Has Pros & Cons

With anything in life, we need to give a balanced view. It's no good telling you that life as a Heyoka empath is going to be all flowers and roses every single day of your life. It's not. There will be days when you feel burdened by the heavy weight of negativity being soaked up from around you, and you'll struggle to understand the emotions that are coming your way. But, by understanding your gift and learning ways to manage it, you'll be able to minimize those downsides and look towards the positives more easily.

In this section, we're going to look at the pros and cons of being a Heyoka empath. However, we should point out that this isn't something you can actually choose. If you're a Heyoka, you're a Heyoka and there's nothing you can do about it. It's part of your fabric, it's who you are. You can deny it and struggle, or you can embrace it and learn to manage it. The latter option is always the better one.

The Benefits of Being a Heyoka

Because we're all about positivity, let's look at the pros of being a Heyoka empath first.

Your Special Ability to Help Other People

Without a doubt, the biggest pro of being a Heyoka empath is your special and unique ability to help other people. You're not just great at giving advice, in fact, that's not something you often do, instead, you're someone who makes people think deeply for themselves. You're a guide, almost a fairy godmother-esque figure who helps them to see things that aren't serving them well and start to make changes.

This is something that you should hold dear to your heart. The ability to help other people in this way is special and there is no bigger pro to your empath gift. Yes, there are downsides, but the very fact that you can change the lives of those around you for the better means that you're one in a million - quite literally.

You Can Learn from The Experiences of Others

It's easy to help someone, move on to the next person, and repeat in a cycle. But, you can also learn from the experience of the people you help. Your life will be full of decisions, choices, ups and downs, and you're going to have problems and issues occasionally, just the same as anyone else. Your ability to help other people doesn't mean that your own life is devoid of problems. But, your experiences in helping others to heal mean that you absorb that knowledge and use it to your own benefit.

Perhaps someone is having a career problem and it's really tying them up in knots. You can feel the heavy sense of negativity around them and their confusion over what to do. You do your Heyoka thing, and you help them, but in the process, you can see the thoughts and ideas flicking through their mind. So, the next time you struggle with your own career and you're not sure which way to turn, remember that experience and see if you can use any of it to help you.

You Can Take Pride in What You Do

Moving on from the first advantage is the fact that your ability to help other people means you can take serious pride in your work. It's a life calling that you have and once you know how to manage it and protect yourself, you can walk around with a very smug smile on your face, knowing that you have one of the most wonderful roles on the planet.

While many people wish they'd done this, or wish they'd said that, you're not likely to have that problem. Your intuition and your keen sense for picking up on energy shifts mean that you literally know what to say at the right time. You're unlikely to make mistakes in this way and that allows you to make a huge difference in the lives of those around you. Take pride in it and wear that smile with glee!

You'll Find it Easier to Solve Problems in Your Own Life

We mentioned that you can use the experiences of those around you to help in your own life but you'll find as part of your Heyoka nature that you're a natural problem solver too. Your keen intuition and your ability to read situations accurately mean that you're not likely to make the wrong move in your own life too often.

All you need to do is think carefully and trust your intuition. At the start, learning how to trust your inner voice and really go along with it can be hard. That's something we're going to talk about in the coming chapters, to help you tap into your powers and really connect with your intuition. But, as you do that, you'll find that problems that come your way are easier to overcome as a result.

You Can Develop Your Confidence and Sense of Self-Worth

It's not hard to feel like you're worth something when you're helping people every day. Your gift as a Heyoka empath means that you're able to guide and teach others and that in itself is a very positive element. You can use that to build your own confidence and your sense of self-worth. Whenever you struggle with negativity and feelings of self-doubt, tell yourself just how amazing you are and what you do for people every day. Create a positive mantra to pull everything back to the forefront of your mind.

In today's negative world, it's all too easy to lack in self-confidence and that leads to feelings of low self-worth. But, you have something in your life that's truly amazing and by remembering it and all the people you've helped, you can boost your confidence levels and arm yourself with all the strength you need to go out and make your life the best it can be.

You Can Use Your Creative Nature in Your Work

Many people want to get into creative careers, but they struggle. These are often jobs that require a natural ability to be creative, to think outside of the box, and to go with your gut. These are all qualities that you have naturally and in abundance!

You will likely be naturally drawn towards a creative career. That might be dancing, singing, drawing, acting, painting, making things in general, e.g., furniture or jewelry, the options are endless. Tapping into your creativity allows you to further connect with your empathic nature and it will also give you a career path that you enjoy and find truly fulfilling. There aren't that many people out there that can hand on heart say that they adore the job they do. Most people go to work to make ends meet. However, when you have a creative job that fulfills you, every day will feel like a joy. That's within your reach.

You Will Develop Your Emotional Intelligence

As you learn how to develop and manage your gift, your emotional intelligence (EQ) level will grow as a welcome side effect. This will allow you to handle your emotions much better but will also help you to observe situations in your life, rather than feeling like you need to act out of panic or worry. Often, this leads to better outcomes and helps you to feel less anxious and worried about your life.

Having a high level of emotional intelligence is useful on many levels. You'll find that you can side-step anger much easier, you'll be able to have better relationships (once you learn to handle your Heyoka tendencies), and you'll feel more positive about your life overall.

Your Ability to Look at Life with Humor

We know that Heyoka empaths tend to use humor to help people shift from a negative to a positive mindset and to start seeing problems and situations in a different light. But your natural sense of humor is also something you can rely upon to help through your own life struggles.

When you laugh at something, yourself, or a problem, everything seems easier to deal with. While there may be times that negativity becomes a little too much (more on how to handle that shortly), if you can maintain that wicked sense of humor that comes to you naturally, you'll find that life's problems are much easier to deal with and much easier to overcome in the short and long-term.

You're Not Likely to be Manipulated by a Liar

Many people fail to understand when someone is being less than faithful or lying to their face. Some people are very good liars and they're able to manipulate and use people without any trace. But a Heyoka empath isn't going to fall foul of this because they can spot a liar from a mile away. Their keen intuition doesn't let anyone with negative intentions get past them and this is definitely one of the biggest advantages of being a Heyoka.

Of course, that doesn't mean it's not hurtful when you realize that someone you perhaps care about has negative intentions. But, it's better than falling foul of a scam that could lead to far more damage later on.

You Can Understand the People in Your Life Very Well

While relationships can be difficult for a Heyoka empath at first, once they learn how to handle their gift, that becomes easier. However, the ability to read people very keenly is one of the main advantages of being a Heyoka.

This can help them to understand their nearest and dearest and avoid potential conflict during difficult times. It's also useful in understanding how they feel - it's likely that a Heyoka isn't going to struggle to know that their partner loves them because they'll feel it radiating from them very easily. This can be reassuring during that early stage in a relationship when nobody knows which way is up or down.

You're Able to Appreciate Nature in a Way That Others Can't

All empaths recharge and destress by spending time alone, but this is doubled when they head out into nature. You're able to appreciate the wonder and serenity of nature in a way that those around you can't. You feel grounded and connected to the elements when you're outside and this helps you to deal with anything that comes your way.

When you go away on vacation, it's a good idea to go to the coast and spend time near the water, perhaps into the mountains, or the countryside. This will help you to disconnect from the maelstrom of emotions around you and help you to reconnect with your true self.

The Negative Aspects of Being a Heyoka

As you can see, there are many fantastic advantages to being a Heyoka empath. The biggest is without a doubt the ability to help people wherever you go. However, it's important to have all sides of the situation so you can understand life as a Heyoka far better. Let's take a look at the negative side of being this very powerful type of empath.

Relationships Can Be Difficult at First

Because an empath can pick up on the emotions of those around them, being in close proximity to someone regularly means that they're likely to connect with their emotions very easily. You may be sitting on the sofa with your partner and you're feeling what they're feeling, perhaps because they've had a bad day at work.

It can be hard to separate your own feelings from theirs in such a close situation. However, by talking to your partner and explaining your empath ways, they will be able to develop a deeper understanding and help you to disconnect. They will understand when you need time alone and you'll slowly be able to learn how to separate your emotions from theirs.

But, not everyone understands and you may find that your partner simply cannot get their head around your empath ways.

You May Feel Overwhelmed in Groups

When you're around more than one person, your sense of feeling overwhelmed will likely grow. The more people, the more you will feel. This makes sense when you go back to basics and look at what happens to an empath - they soak up the emotions of those around them like a sponge. So, the more people, the more soaking that goes on, and soon the sponge becomes saturated to the point where it can't absorb anymore. That's what happens to the empath.

While Heyoka empaths are usually introverted (not always) and they do enjoy time alone, there is also that desire to socialize too. This can be hard because of the fact that they're likely to feel overwhelmed after a short amount of time. It can certainly cause problems in their social life and within their circle of friends. As such, many empaths overall, not just Heyokas, usually have just one or two very close friends they trust and socialize with.

It Can be Upsetting When People Don't Know How to React to You/Trust You

Heyoka empaths do not walk into situations with calm and serenity. Their main focus is to disrupt and shake up the energy to get a person to see problems and start to explore different ways forward. Within this, it's possible that many people may simply not know how to react to the empath. They may feel a deep distrust or even a dislike for their satirical humor. Of course, we know that the humor is never meant negatively, it's designed to help the person. Until they understand this, it's possible that people react to you differently or negatively.

It can be hard to deal with but it's something that you'll learn to reframe and understand as time goes on. Always remember that your main focus is to help people heal, yet you cannot force them to see their problems if they don't want to be open to them.

You're Misunderstood Easily

Heyoka empaths often feel like they don't fit in generally but it's probably the case that you simply feel misunderstood much of the time. Again, this can be difficult to deal with because everyone wants to be liked and nobody wants to be thought of as 'different' simply because people don't understand them.

As before, it's possible that you want to have a strong social circle and you want to enjoy time with others but your gift stands in the way of that happening. It's not likely to be possible for a Heyoka empath to ever be able to stand in a large group of people and never be affected at all.

You May Not Understand Your Gift and Struggle at First

Before you come to realize that you are indeed a Heyoka empath, it's possible that you will simply struggle to understand what is going on. You might assume that something is wrong with you and struggle with the fact that you always feel like you don't quite fit in.

Life can be quite chaotic and extremely negative for an empath that is "undiagnosed". However, once you realize that you're an empath, you can start to put in place strategies to protect yourself against negativity and learn how to handle your gift. Before that point, life may be a little up and down for a while.

You Absorb a Lot of Negativity

You're made up of light energy and the dark energy that you absorb from those around you who are struggling with negative emotions and situations. As such, you will often find that your mind goes towards the negative side of the equation, simply because you're full of darker energy at times. It goes without saying that living your life surrounded by negativity never more than a few feet away is likely to make you feel quite down from time to time.

It's important to learn how to shed that negativity and focus on positive light as an empath. It can be hard at first, but with practice and knowledge, you'll understand what you need to do and you'll learn the signs that it's time to head out into nature and declutter your mind.

You Take a Lot of Things to Heart

This point continues on from the idea that the Heyoka empath may often be misunderstood or thought of as 'different' in ways they don't want to be. As such, if someone doesn't trust you or doesn't know how to react to you, it may cause you to feel upset and to take it to heart. You're very sensitive in general, which is a slightly unpleasant side effect of having such a strong intuition.

As such, unless you learn to build up a wall of defense against such situations, you're probably going to find yourself feeling regularly hurt emotionally. That type of overwhelming negativity can drag you down if you allow it to.

Your Moods Often Swing from One to The Other

Some people report that Heyoka empaths have bipolar tendencies but that doesn't mean that they're more likely to develop the condition. It's another way of saying that moods can often swing from one extreme to the other when surrounded by a lot of negativity and difficult situations. Of course, when left unchecked this could lead to you feeling extremely down and perhaps even towards depression if you allow it to continue.

Sometimes you may not understand the difference between your own emotions and those of the people around you, especially if you're relatively new to your empath gifts. But, as your emotional intelligence grows, your ability to control your emotions will increase too. This reduces the risk of any adverse effects on your mental health.

Your Time Management Issues Can Make Life Difficult

We already mentioned earlier on in our traits section that many Heyoka empaths struggle with time management. This can cause you problems in general life but also at work. Your tendency to feel overwhelmed or negative at times can hold you back and it's important to have some kind of structure or routine that keeps you on track as much as possible and to stop you from encountering issues when you need to be somewhere, or you need to complete something by a specific time.

As you can see, there is a relatively even balance of pros and cons when it comes to life as a Heyoka empath. However, the main pro - the ability to help others - should be what keeps you ticking along. You can learn to mitigate the negatives and cut out the effects on your life by learning how to handle your gift and how to know when you're starting to feel overwhelmed with negative energy and emotions around you.

Again, that's something we're going to focus on very soon.

The Crucial Role of Positivity in Your Life

You'll notice that we've used the word 'negativity' a lot in this chapter, in fact, throughout the whole book. Whether we want to admit it or not, the world is full of negativity and as a Heyoka empath, you're drawn to people who are struggling, because it's your role to help them heal.

We've also mentioned several times that being surrounded by negativity can be extremely difficult and can, if you allow it to, drag you down and cause you to struggle with your mood a lot. But, it doesn't have to be that way.

What is the opposite of negativity?

Positivity obviously!

By doing your best to hold onto the positive elements in your life and by learning how to foster a positive mindset, you'll find that you're able to knock negativity on its side when it comes your way. That doesn't mean you're never going to feel overwhelmed, because that's part and parcel of being an empath. But by learning ways to reduce that, you can stop it from taking over your life.

Learning how to become more positive means learning two specific strategies. However, simply keeping positivity in the forefront of your mind and visualizing positive outcomes is a good route forward too. That's not to say that you'll find it easy to shrug off negativity when it comes your way. After all, as a Heyoka empath, you're a caring and deeply intuitive person. It's not possible for you to be unaffected by negative situations around you, because you end up caring about the people you help.

50

While it's not the most positive thing to feel at the time, try your best to reframe it (more on that shortly) to understand just how special it is to be able to do that for people.

The two strategies we're going to talk about when it comes to arming yourself with a more positive mindset are reframing and positive mantras.

Reframing Negatives into Positives

The first strategy for maintaining a positive mindset is to reframe any negative thought you have into a positive one. Whenever an emotion comes over you, try to pinpoint what it is. Acknowledge the feeling and give it a name, such as 'anger', 'sadness', 'frustration'.

As you're soaking up emotions from those around you, you may not be aware of what's causing that situation, but by reading the person, you're probably going to be able to put the pieces together to come up with a rough idea. Even though the situation isn't yours to deal with, the emotion is now upon you. So, take the emotion and the potential cause and find a positive.

Let's give a rough example of how reframing works and you can then take the idea and adapt it to the negative situations you encounter as you go about your daily life.

Let's say that it's raining, and it's been raining for many days. You're tired of the rain and you really want some sun. You're feeling a little down and frustrated because you can't get out and do what you want to do.

The first step is to acknowledge the emotion, so you're frustrated. Then you need to identify the negative thought. In this case, it's 'I hate the rain'. The thought is negative because it's causing you to feel a negative emotion (frustration) and it uses negative language, e.g., 'hate'.

Now, you need to come up with a positive twist on that statement. This will be easier with some thoughts than others. In this case, you can say 'When the rain stops I'm going to go for a long walk in the countryside'. That way, you have something to look forward to and you're turning the negative into a positive. You could also say something like 'I enjoy the smell of rain'.

The next point in reframing is an important one - repetition.

Repetition is how the brain learns. You might remember when you were in school and learning the alphabet. Your teacher made you sing the alphabet song over and over again. At the time, it may have been annoying, but have you ever forgotten it? No. The reason? Repetition.

When you repeat something over and over, the brain commits it to the long-term memory bank, and it becomes your go-to thought for that particular situation. So, if you repeat your reframed positive thought enough times and visualize it to give it extra power, whenever you see rain in the future, you'll think of the positive thought and not the negative one.

Will it happen overnight? No. You need to keep repeating it and you need to mean what you're saying. You have to do all you can to try and believe the positive. You might have a few false starts but that's fine. Nobody masters reframing on the first try.

The point is you keep going and you will, eventually, notice that your thoughts move towards the positive end of the scale more than the negative. As an empath, you're always going to be surrounded by a certain amount of negative, especially as a Heyoka. However, by having a strategy such as reframing at your disposal, you'll find that you can mitigate some of the effects.

Using Positive Mantras

Anyone can use a positive mantra and get plenty of benefit out of it, but as a Heyoka empath, positive mantras are even more important. You can use a mantra at any time; you don't have to be feeling negative to make use of this strategy.

A mantra is a statement you choose that sums up how you want to feel. The trick is to really believe it to be real. Of course, it has to be positive too.

For instance, if you're struggling with negative emotions, your positive mantra could be "I am positive and I have hope", "I am strong and I can handle anything that comes my way", "I am a healer, and I am helping those around me", etc. It can be anything. You can head online and find a few suggestions, or you can come up with your own. But, the mantra you choose has to resonate with what you want to feel and believe. You also have to put your entire being into it and really believe it to be true. Then, the more you repeat it (that strategy again), the easier your brain will trigger into thinking that it indeed is the truth.

Once you've chosen your mantra, and make sure you give plenty of thought to your choice, repeat it three times in the morning when you wake up. Close your eyes, visualize it being true, and really feel the words as you say them aloud. It's best to say them verbally and not just think them as that helps them to feel more real. Then, repeat your mantra again at the halfway point of the day, and again before bed. You can also repeat your mantra at any point when you feel your resolve weakening a little.

It's a good idea to write your mantra down and keep it somewhere you can see it, such as your bathroom mirror, your laptop screen, or even your phone home screen.

Your mantra won't become second nature to you immediately, but the more you repeat it, the easier it will be for you to feel the word you're saying to yourself. As with reframing, over time, the more your brain will go to that mantra as the first thing it believes to be true.

Positivity is something we all need to focus on, empath or not. But, life as an empath can be drowning in negativity if you allow it to really get to you. These two strategies will help you to focus on becoming more positive overall but will also give you a go-to approach when you feel like negativity is starting to swim all around you.

Remember, negativity is a choice at the end of the day, and you're well within your rights to choose positivity instead.

Embrace The Uniqueness of Your Empathic Nature

Whenever you read anything about empaths, it's also peppered with a lot of talk about how it can be a difficult life and how you need to protect yourself and learn to manage the situation. That's 100% true and something we can't get away from. It's simply part and parcel of being an empath.

There is no good in the world without a little bad. There is no positivity without a small amount of skepticism or negativity. But, you can choose to be more positive and you can choose to see the light more than the darkness.

Being an empath is a wonderful gift. It's something you should embrace, hold close to you, and really cherish as a major part of your life. The empath within you is part of you. It's a thread that runs through your personality and your entire being. You can't choose to take time off or to push it to one side - it's who you are.

Your only choice is to embrace it. Hold that empath part of you close and learn to love it. Yes, sometimes it's hard, but overall, you're blessed to have a gift that can change people's lives.

Of course, you want things to be easier and that's understandable. In the next chapter we're going to talk at great length about how you can make your life as a Heyoka empath much easier and then, you can focus your attention on helping others while avoiding the major downsides of life as an empath.

Points to Remember

This chapter has been another long one but packed with information you need to take on board. There is no good in life without the bad, but that is what makes it so wonderful. The same goes for your empathic gift. Being a Heyoka empath means you have great power, but it also comes at a cost - the risk of being overwhelmed with negativity and too many emotions flying at you at one time.

There are pros and cons to being a Heyoka empath, but the good news is that the negative elements have ways to mitigate the damage. That means you can focus on the positives and not have quite so much of an impact thrown your way.

We've also talked about how you need to focus on having a positive mindset as a Heyoka. Negativity will be all around you, and when it's not in your direct line of vision or feeling, you'll know that it's never too far away. You read energies automatically - you don't get to pick and choose who comes your way. But, you can learn how to focus on a more positive mindset and that will help you to push aside negativity that simply doesn't belong to you.

Reframing negative thoughts into positive news and using positive mantras are both very useful and highly successful ways to develop a more positive mindset in general. These are things you can start to practice right now! In our next chapter, we're going to talk about how you can improve your life even more. You might need to take notes, and you're certainly going to need to move slowly through the points so you can try them all out and find out what works best for you. But, the point is, there is a lot of positivity and light on the horizon - not only for the people you help, but for you too.

Chapter 5:
Protect Yourself And Set Boundaries as a Heyoka Empath

Now we're about to move onto a really proactive and practical chapter!

The last few chapters have been designed to give you a large amount of information about the Heyoka empath. There was a very good reason for that - you need to know what you're dealing with and that will help you to identify for sure whether you're a Heyoka or not. You also need to arrive at a positive point of view when it comes to seeing life as this powerful type of empath too.

By this point, you should be pretty clear on your stance. Either you're quite sure you're a Heyoka and you want to learn how to manage your gift, or you think you're a different type of empath and you still want to know if you can glean any help from the Heyoka on how to deal with your own gift. Of course, it could be that you're not an empath at all but you're just highly fascinated with the subject. The good news is that Heyoka, another type of empath, or none at all, there is plenty of advice to read in this coming chapter that will help you to become a calmer, less stressed, and more emotionally balanced person.

Learning how to manage your gift is vital. Being a Heyoka is wonderful, truly, but if you don't learn how to protect yourself and know when you're feeling overwhelmed, negativity will eat you up for dinner.

That's not going to happen, because you have a world of strategies to learn in the coming sections.

The Importance of Serenity & Calm

In the coming sections, you're going to learn a lot about how to manage your gift. Take your time and work through them one by one. You might find that some work better for you than others. That's fine - we're all different and there is no 'one size fits all' answer here. It might also help you to take notes as we go through. But you can always come back to these sections and go back over anything you want to try as you move through the strategies one by one.

The first thing we're going to talk about is why it's important to be calm and serene, and how you can move towards doing that as a regular part of your life.

Your Heyoka gift is designed to shake things up, disturb the energies around you, and detected negativity whenever it arises around you. That means that life is probably going to feel pretty chaotic at times. Your mind is likely to feel like it's racing, and you have many different emotions heading your way, many of which aren't your own.

When you have that type of situation going on, the perfect antidote is the opposite - the opposite of chaos is calm.

Calmness and serenity help you to let go of the emotions that you've absorbed, and it allows you to shed away the negativity that you might have encountered. You can reconnect with your own emotions when you're free from the emotions of other people flying all around you. That's why spending time alone is so important for empaths. It's something they crave and it's probably the case for you too.

Let's take a look at some ways you can seek calmness and serenity as a Heyoka empath and reconnect with your own emotions.

Enjoy Your Own Company

We just mentioned spending time alone and this is an important one. Many people falsely believe spending time alone means that you're lonely but that's not the case at all. We all need to spend some time alone because it helps us reconnect with who we are and gives us the time we need to focus on our goals and dreams. If you're always around other people, you're never going to have the time to think about the things you want in life. You'll always be following the crowd.

At first, it may be difficult to spend time alone, but as an empath, you probably crave the time spent in calmness on some level. The more time you spend with yourself, the more you'll come to realize that actually, you're pretty good company! You don't have to compromise, disagree, or pretend you're listening - you can do exactly what you want, and you don't have to bend even halfway to anyone else's will.

For Heyoka empaths, in fact, any empath at all, spending time alone is key to a calm and happy life. We've already mentioned the fact that most empaths do not like spending time in large groups of people. If they find themselves in this type of situation, they're likely to find an excuse to extract themselves and move on pretty quickly. Once that happens, they need to retreat to their own shell for a while.

If you're not doing plenty of this, you need to start. That doesn't mean isolating yourself and never spending time with others, but it does mean learning to enjoy your own company. Choose some hobbies that you love, preferably something creative. Spend time just focusing on what you want, be it sitting in a warm bubble bath, reading, or simply listening to your favorite music.

Spending time alone gives you the chance to regroup and if you don't do that, you're going to be carrying a lot of emotions around with you, ones that simply don't belong to you in the first place.

Try Essential Oils For Relaxation

Achieving a state of calmness and serenity means that you need to relax and that's not something that comes easily to everyone. We're all so focused upon running from one task to the next, trying to tick times off our to-do list that we forgot to stop and calm down. As an empath, you need that more than anyone else.

We know that you need to spend some time alone, xcccccbut you can combine that with the use of essential oils too.

Essential oils are extracted from plants and flowers, therefore maintaining a lot of their natural healing elements. When used in the correct way, they're known to help balance and calm you down. They also interact with the limbic system in the brain, which is known to be the emotional center. When the scent from the essential oil makes its way from the nose and affects the limbic system, it quickly calms you down, soothes your problems, and helps to regulate emotions that may be running wild. That's exactly what an empath needs to do in order to achieve a state of calm and tranquility on a regular basis.

Essential oils act quickly and they're suitable for most people also do check with your doctor beforehand if you're not sure. There are some contraindications and it's better to be safe, rather than sorry.

The best essential oils for grounding and calming (exactly what an empath needs) are:

- Lavender
- Lemon
- Vetiver

- Frankincense
- Marjoram
- Rosemary
- Jasmine
- Chamomile
- Sage
- Black spruce

There are several ways you can use essential oils. The first way is to use a diffuser and simply sit somewhere calm and smell the beautiful scent of the oil. This will quickly help you to feel grounded, you'll notice that negativity and negative emotions drift away, and your mood will be lifted. You can also sniff directly from the bottle if you don't have a diffuser, or you want to feel calmer quickly when you're out and about. This is good when you're outside, enjoy the calming effects of nature too.

Another option is to apply topically to the pressure points, including the temples and wrists. However, if you're going to apply any essential oil to your skin, make sure that you dilute it first with a carrier oil, such as coconut oil, olive oil, or jojoba oil as a few examples.

You can also add a few drops of diluted essential oils to your bathwater. This works on several levels. Firstly, you're enjoying the generally relaxing feel of the warmth from the water, but you're also in water which is a natural element and is automatically calming. Then, the relaxation from the scent of the oil will add to the benefit.

The final option is to use a humidifier but do check that your humidifier can accommodate essential oils, as not all can.

Spend Time in Nature

Mother Nature has you covered! Have you noticed that when you go outside into the fresh air, you feel instantly better? There's a reason for that. Fresh air and natural light have been shown time and time again to improve mood and allow us to calm down from difficult situations.

For instance, if you're feeling angry, it's far better to take five minutes away from the situation and go outside into the fresh air, than to stay in the room. You'll find that five minutes outside will quickly calm you down. For sure, you may still be extremely annoyed about whatever happened, but your feelings will abate and you'll side-step a reaction that could probably end up being quite damaging.

As a Heyoka empath, you need to spend as much time outdoors as you can. That doesn't mean getting soaked in the rain, but it does mean dedicating at least some of your time during the day to being at one with nature. That sounds quite 'out there' but try it and you'll see exactly what we mean. The ability to ground yourself and feel far more in your own emotional sphere is much easier done when you're surrounded by the elements. There's something about the wind blowing around you, the sun on your skin, and the cold chill hitting your face that is rejuvenating on many levels. Even the sounds - the sea gently lapping or even crashing against the shore, the sound of the birds in the sky, the leaves of a tree rustling in the breeze, or the wind howling across the hills and mountains. These are all ultra-calming and grounding things to which empaths will feel drawn.

If you're feeling like you have a need to get outside, listen to it. It's your intuition telling you that you need to regroup, and nature is the very best way to do that.

Exercise

You might wonder what is relaxing about exercise. After all, it gets your blood pumping, and you end up all sweaty! However, exercise has consistently been connected with improved mood and emotional balance. That doesn't mean you need to join the gym and hit the treadmill, although you can do that if you are drawn to it. Instead, you could think about going for a jog around the local park, going outside for a walk with your dog, or trying yoga.

Yoga is a particularly good option for empaths as it connects to your breath - the most grounding thing you can possibly do. You're also pulled to the present moment, mindful of not only your breath but the sounds around you and the feelings within your body.

If you've never tried yoga before, it's actually easier to start than you might think. Don't be put off by gravity-defying poses you see on the Internet - there are many different types of yoga and you can start with something mild and less technical! There are also yoga types and different poses if you struggle with a particular injury, e.g., back pain, and you can do yoga when you're pregnant, as long as you modify the poses you're doing to avoid causing harm or extra strain.

If you're not someone who exercises regularly, it's time to add this to your regular routine. Not only does exercise help to keep your heart healthy but it does a lot for your mind too. As a Heyoka empath, you need to strengthen your defenses against negativity as much as possible and exercise will give you a healthy outlet to push away negativity and focus upon grounding yourself in your own emotions and within your own body. You'll also feel a sense of confidence and happiness that you're doing something for yourself and for your general health too.

Look at Your Diet

This one might sound strange but bear with us. Your digestive health is quite heavily connected to your mental health.

Think back to the last time you struggled with a stomach upset - did you feel upbeat and positive? No, you probably felt down and quite miserable. We're learning more and more about the gut-brain connection and there are certain foods you may be eating that are upsetting that connection and causing you to feel unlike yourself, or more focused on negativity.

As an empath, you need to keep yourself grounded and calm as much as possible and if you're not healthy on the inside, that's not going to be easy to do.

When your intestines aren't happy, e.g., you're eating something they don't like or you've overeaten/undereaten, they send a signal to the brain. The same goes in a vice versa situation - when you're feeling anxious or depressed, your appetite and digestive health are affected too.

If you find that your stomach is often bloated, or you simply don't feel like your digestive health is the best, that could be affecting your ability to handle emotions and your general mood. Keep a food journal for a few weeks and try and pinpoint what foods cause you to feel that particular way. Then, cut them out of your diet and see how you feel. You can then slowly reintroduce them and see if they have any effect, until you find your happy level.

You might also find some benefit from speaking to your doctor about possible food sensitivities and intolerances. Many people struggle with a gluten intolerance, soy, or lactose, and these are all possible reasons for a gut and mood issue combined.

If nothing else, cutting out junk food, eating a healthy and balanced diet, and making sure that you get a good amount of fresh fruit and vegetables will help you to feel better on the inside. That will give you a lot more strength to handle the challenges that your Heyoka nature throws at you.

Use Deep Breathing Exercises

Your breath is the one thing that is present and with you from the moment you're born, until the moment you die. It never leaves you; it never lets you down, and it always reminds you of the very fact that you're alive. As such, connecting with your breath is the ultimate grounding tool and something you can use to calm yourself down, reconnect with your own emotions, and achieve a sense of calm and tranquility.

Deep breathing exercises can be done anywhere, but if you can sit outdoors and connect with nature, you'll find more benefit. Of course, you need to make sure that you're somewhere you're not going to be disturbed, and that means turning off your phone and locking your door.

Some specific exercises are ideal for empaths. Let's take a look at a few you can practice.

Deep Breathing Exercise 1

You can do this exercise anywhere, but it's better to be sat or laid down. However, if you're outdoors and you need to calm or ground yourself quickly, you can simply excuse yourself and try this on the go. It's perfect for taking the sting out of an extreme emotion, especially anxiety or anger.

- Sit somewhere comfortably, or lay down if you prefer
- Make sure you're warm enough, or not too warm and that nothing is going to distract you, such as too-tight clothing, etc
- Close your eyes and when you're ready, take a deep breath in through your nose for a slow count of five
- Hold the breath for a slow count of two
- Exhale through your mouth slowly and steadily, for a count of five

- Hold the breath for another slow count of two
- Repeat the exercise for ten rounds, or until you feel calmer
- When you're ready, slowly open your eyes and remain still for a few minutes, before you move.

Deep Breathing Exercise 2

When you're anxious or stressed, you will start to breathe in a more shallow manner. This means your breathing becomes faster and you'll breathe from the chest, rather than the abdomen. By focusing upon correcting that issue, you'll find that you automatically calm yourself and feel more grounded in the moment.

- Sit in an upright (yet comfortable) position, or lie down flat
- Make sure that you're comfortable before you begin
- Place one hand on your abdomen, just below your belly button, and the other hand on your chest, where you're currently breathing from
- When you're ready, take a deep breath through your nose, directing the breath down to your belly, so the hand beneath your belly button rises. Make sure that the hand on your chest stays still
- Wait for a second and then push the breath out through pursed lips, making a 'whooshing' sound as you do so. The hand on your belly should flatten back down and you can also gently apply a very small amount of pressure to push the air back out again
- Repeat the process up to ten times, making sure that you don't rush
- Once you're finished, remain still for a few seconds before moving.

Deep Breathing Exercise 3

The third exercise we're going to talk about is called the 4-7-8 technique and it has its roots in yogic breathing, known as pranayama. This is an ancient technique that has been shown to calm and reduce anxiety, while also grounding.

This exercise can be done up to two times per day when you first start, and you can slowly build up to four times over time. The reason is that at first, you might notice that you feel a little lightheaded but as you get used to the exercise and build up your technique, that should ease.

- Sit in a comfortable chair, making sure that your back is straight
- Move your tongue so that it sits behind your top teeth
- Feel comfortable in the position before you begin
- Empty your lungs of all breath by exhaling through your mouth, keeping your tongue in position - you'll notice that it makes a 'whooshing' noise
- Once you've exhaled, close your mouth and breath in through your nose for a slow count of four
- Now, for a slow and steady count of seven, hold your breath
- Repeat the mouth exhalation, with your tongue remaining in place, for a slow and steady count of eight
- Repeat the process three more times.

These breathing exercises are ideal for when you start to feel a heightened emotion, especially one that is not your own. As you detect negative energies around you, extract yourself from the situation and focus on your breath. When you do that, you'll notice that you become instantly calmer and grounded in the moment.

Learning to feel calmer and tranquil will benefit you in the long run. But, it's also something you can use when you notice fast-approaching emotions that threaten to send you into a tailspin.

Of course, your Heyoka nature means that you want to help other people, but that doesn't mean you should always put your own needs last. There will be times when you simply want to lock yourself away and destress. If you feel the need to do that, listen to your body. These techniques give you something to keep to yourself and use whenever necessary. Consider them your magical toolbox of tricks!

Signs You're Close to Emotional Burnout

It can be very easy for Heyoka empaths to experience emotional exhaustion or burnout. This is the point when you simply can't absorb any more emotions and your quota for negativity is reaching its full point.

It's important to understand the signs that this is happening. Of course, it's important to avoid getting to this point in the first place, but sometimes you will work to help people a little too much and forget to recognize your own health and wellbeing at the same time.

You're a healer. You're someone who naturally wants to give a helping hand to those around you. If anything, it's your calling and something you can't deny.

But, there comes a time when you have to come first. After all, if you don't help yourself, how are you going to help other people? When you're emotionally exhausted, you literally don't have the capacity to take on any further load. You can't help anyone else because you're full up to the brim. You need to let out some of that emotional load to be able to feel better and then start to help others once more.

Put simply, you need to help yourself as a priority and that's something most of us find difficult to do. When you're a Heyoka empath, your caring nature makes it ten times harder to put yourself first. But, it's time.

Anyone can approach emotional exhaustion. You don't have to be an empath to feel this way. If you're someone reading this book who isn't sure if you're an empath or you're just reading for total interest, you can use this section in your own life regardless. Emotional exhaustion comes when we take on too much, we try to help too much, or life just throws us far too much to deal with.

As a Heyoka empath, the amount of energy you feel around you from day to day can be quite exhausting. It's not only about learning how to manage your gift and protect yourself from overload, it's about understanding when that point of a crash is on the horizon and doing something about it.

A few common signs that you're approaching emotional exhaustion or burnout include:

- Feeling frustrated and as though you're unable to move in any direction
- Irritability with those around you, including your own abilities
- You can't focus and concentrate on anything, at least not for very long
- You start to feel numb to emotions because you can't absorb them anymore
- A sense of pessimism, even about things that normally excite you
- You're starting to withdraw from friendships and relationships to spend more and more time alone
- You're struggling with anxiety
- You're sleeping a lot, or not sleeping too much at all
- You might feel depressed, or be struggling with low mood generally

It's important to recognize the signs so that you can intervene and stop the situation from worsening. As before, anyone can feel emotionally overwhelmed and exhausted but as a Heyoka, you're far more likely to reach this point than anyone else.

Journaling is a good route here. By keeping a journal and recording how you feel, you'll be able to recognize any signs that may otherwise slip through the net. You don't have to write full paragraphs or even sentences. You simply need to write down words that mean something to you. Then, you can identify how you feel from day to day and any notable events that occurred. By connecting events to your feelings, you'll be able to recognize when you're approaching the point of being overwhelmed.

This will be slightly different for everyone, which is why journaling is such a good choice. There are common signs but what about your own personal signs? How can you tell what your intuition and your body are trying to tell you if you're not aware of what to look for?

Reflect on your journal regularly and you'll gain a lot of benefit from it.

Taking The Time To Be There For Yourself

Learning your own personal signs of emotional exhaustion is important but you also need to know how vital it is to take time out for yourself.

Again, we tend to think that looking after number one is selfish. But how can it be? If you're not strong within yourself and if you don't understand how important you are, how can you expect anyone else to do the same?

As a Heyoka, you place so much importance upon everyone else. It's likely that you don't feel like spending time on yourself is worthwhile, but that's completely untrue. As we said before, if you don't look after yourself, you're not going to be in a position to help anyone else. But, even more importantly, you need to feel healthy and well for yourself anyway.

You're important.

Yes, you have a wonderful gift to help other people but that's not everything you are. You're an individual who needs to focus on your own needs and desires occasionally. You're someone who has to make sure that they're feeling good, that they're healthy, and their basic needs are met.

You cannot deny your empathic side, but you also need to look after your human side. If you don't do that, you'll find that emotional exhaustion is the least of your worries as that can quickly turn to darker routes. Negativity can take hold to the point where it requires a lot of time and effort to drag yourself out. Nobody wants to invite depression and anxiety into their lives but when you become emotionally burnt out, that's a fast track towards poor mental health.

Taking time out for yourself doesn't have to mean anything major. It can be as simple as watching your favorite movie at the end of a long day. Maybe it's ordering your favorite takeaway meal or cooking your favorite pasta. It could be rewarding yourself with a huge bar of chocolate (moderation, of course), or enjoying a long, hot bubble bath with candles to boot.

Taking time out for yourself just means doing things that you enjoy. Everyone's choices will be different because we all enjoy different things. But, as a Heyoka empath, looking towards creative endeavors is a good idea. You can press yourself through creative means and channel your emotions and your frustrations in positive ways.

It's important to make sure that you avoid venting your frustrations through negative channels. When people struggle to deal with something, it's easy to go down the path of vice. For instance, turning to drink, smoking, eating too much, not eating at all, shopping, overexercising, or even taking drugs. These aren't things that will help your health and wellbeing and they will do nothing for your empathic nature either.

So, as easy as it can be to slip towards the darkness when things feel too much, always focus on the light.

Getting a Good Night of Sleep

In modern society, we tend to reward ourselves for doing everything all at once. We place rest and sleep right at the bottom of our priority list and we just keep going until we crash. That's not healthy.

As an empath, you need to rest, and you need to be strong to face another day. Sleep will help you to do that.

Did you know that just one night of poor sleep can affect you for several days afterward? You end up in a sleep debt and it must be paid back. When it isn't, you continue to feel groggy, irritable, low in energy, your appetite is all over the place, and you can't focus. This simply worsens if your sleep problem continues.

As a Heyoka empath, you may struggle with sleep from time to time. This is a common issue and something which you should focus on to help strengthen your resolve and deal with any health issues that may come your way.

Never underestimate the power of sleep. You cannot handle whatever life throws at you if you're not well-rested. Your body needs you to sleep so that it can heal and regenerate. Your brain needs you to rest so it can deal with whatever you've handled throughout the day. Without all this, you're starting another day on a very rocky foundation indeed.

In this section, we're going to give you a few handy hints on how you can focus on getting a better night's sleep. A lot of this information is useful for everyone, not just Heyoka empaths, but it's important to remember that for an empath, sleep can be a major issue. When you're not firing on all cylinders within yourself, you have zero chance of helping anyone or protecting yourself against negativity.

To encourage a good night's sleep on a regular basis, follow these sleep hygiene tips.

- **Have a regular sleep schedule** - Make sure that you get up at the same time every day and go to bed at the same time. This will help to set your circadian rhythm (body clock) and help you get into a better sleep routine.
- **Avoid stimulants before bed** - Caffeine, cola, chocolate, loud music, action or horror films, video games, these are all things you should avoid in the hours before bed. They will simply get your adrenaline pumping and you'll find it harder to nod off to sleep.
- **Avoid heavy food before bed** - If you're going to have anything before bed, make it a milky drink. Large amounts of water or heavy food in the hours before you intend to sleep will mean that your digestive system is working overtime and you'll struggle to sleep
- **Have a warm bath** - Don't have the water too hot, but a warm bath before bed may help you to relax and fall asleep faster. Again, you could try lavender essential oil in your bathroom (diluted).
- **Try lavender essential oil** - We mentioned the use of essential oils for relaxation and grounding earlier but lavender oil, in particular, is very good for helping you to unwind before bed. Try a pillow mist or apply diluted lavender oil (with a carrier) oil to your pressure points. Some people find that diluted lavender oil on the soles of their feet helps too.
- **Have a relaxation schedule** - Set a schedule of relaxation exercises that you carry out before you sleep. That could include the bath we just mentioned, but you could also write

in your journal so that you're offloading any information or emotions before you sleep, meditate, or try deep breathing exercises.

- **Keep a notebook by the side of your bed** - Many people wake up and remember something and then struggle to sleep afterward because they worry they'll forget it. Keep a notebook at the side of your bed and then you can scribble anything down and get it out of your mind.
- **Try meditation before bed** - We're going to talk about meditation shortly and give you a few exercises to try but meditation before bed will help to ground you and allow you to be totally relaxed before you sleep.
- **Don't have your phone or TV in the bedroom** - Technology doesn't belong in your bedroom. This should be your haven of relaxation. Many people lie in bed on their phones, but this disrupts their sleep. If you really have to use your phone, make sure you put it onto night mode so that the blue light isn't going to affect your sleep.
- **Avoid strong smells in your bedroom** - As an empath, you're particularly sensitive to smells so if you have any scented candles or anything particularly strong-smelling, remove them from your bedroom otherwise they will simply disrupt your sleep.
- **Try white noise** - You can buy a white noise machine if you want to but there are many free apps you can download and use. Of course, that means having your phone in the room and if you are going to do that, make sure that it's on night mode and you don't feel tempted to pick it up and start scrolling through social media at night.
- **Try a weighted blanket** - Weighted blankets are truly relaxing and can help you to drift off and stay asleep more easily. Originally used for people with restless legs syndrome, these blankets are designed to help the brain release the relaxing hormone, oxytocin. The slight pressure from the weight feels like a hug, and this is what encourages

74

the hormone release. As such, you're more likely to feel sleepy.

- **Check the temperature of the room** - If your room is too hot or cold, you'll struggle to sleep, especially as you're someone who is quite sensitive anyway. Have a window open slightly if you feel a little warm, but make sure that you avoid sleeping with the heating on as this will just make the room stuffy.
- **Make sure your bed is comfortable** - This one may seem obvious, but you would be surprised at the number of people who have had the same pillows for years! Pillows lose their support after a while and can cause neck pain or general discomfort. Make sure that you change your pillows at least every year and check your bedding to make sure that the fabric isn't scratchy against your skin. You need to be as comfortable as possible whilst you're in bed.

These tips will help you to focus on getting a good night's sleep. However, if you still find that you're struggling, it may be a good idea to talk to your doctor. Many empaths struggle with insomnia some of the time and there are treatments that may help you to minimize sleep disruption. Melatonin patches are a good choice if you prefer to go down the natural route but a conversation with your doctor will highlight the best options for your situation.

10 Ways to Protect Your Heyoka Gift

We've talked about how you can ensure a sense of calmness and tranquility but it's important to have some protection strategies ready to go too. Negative energy may arise at any point and in some cases, this may be quite extreme. Protection helps you to avoid absorbing excessive amounts of this energy and also helps you to shed the energy when you feel like it's getting to be too much.

In this section, we're going to cover some easy-to-follow protection exercises. Some will require a little practice; others are things you can do immediately. Work through them all and see which ones work best for you. As before, not everything will work for you straight away or at all. Every Heyoka empath is different. What works for you may not work for the next Heyoka. Find your go-to strategies and whenever you feel like you're starting to feel heavy with negativity and emotion, use them to protect you and move towards the light.

Journalling

We've talked about journaling for a few situations already but it's a protection strategy too. When you write down how you feel, it's a cathartic procedure. You're literally transferring thoughts from your brain, down your arms, to your hands, and onto the paper where you're writing. It's a good idea to actually physically write your journal and not type. If you prefer, you can do it, but the physical act of writing words helps you to get everything out.

Again, you can use paragraphs, sentences, or just words - whatever works best for you. Journaling before bed is a good choice because it gets everything out of your mind before you rest for the evening. However, you can keep your journal with you and scribble in it whenever you need to. Your journal will also prove to be a valuable tool for identifying triggers and patterns.

Practice Mindfulness

Mindfulness is very important for empaths. It's very easy to start living in the past or jumping forward to the future, but it's vital that you learn how to live in the present moment. This will help you to deal with anything that comes your way and stop pushing things to one side, bottling things up, or allowing everything to build up into a crescendo of emotions.

Being mindful isn't going to happen overnight but with practice, you will learn how to stay in the here and now far more easily. There are some very easy meditation exercises you can do, such as walking mindfulness meditation or simply trying mindful eating.

Mindful eating is probably the easiest way to begin. Most of us rush through our food and we don't take the time to enjoy it. As such, we tend to eat too much and end up with digestive issues. When you eat mindfully, you slow down and appreciate the moment you're in, including the textures, tastes, and feeling of eating.

- Sit down at the table with your meal and before you eat, look at the food you're going to eat. Notice the presentation, the colors, the shapes, etc.
- When you're ready to eat, take your first mouthful and chew ten times. Make sure your chewing is slow and deliberate
- As you chew, notice the way the food feels in your mouth, the texture, and the flavors as they burst on your tastebuds
- When you're ready to swallow, do so deliberately and notice how it feels. Take note of the way your throat constricts as the food travels down your throat and any lingering tastes and flavors
- Take a second before you repeat the process
- As you eat, be mindful of how your stomach feels. Do you feel full? Are you still hungry? The idea is to eat until you're just full and not to overfill your stomach, making you feel sluggish and heavy
- Once you've finished eating, take a second to give thanks for your food, and don't rush off to do whatever else is on your to-do list. Sit for a second and notice how you feel - satiated and calm.

You could also try the aforementioned walking mindful meditation. This is another easy option to try and it's not the regular type of meditation that you would think of. Walking meditation involves heading outside somewhere quiet and calm, perhaps the park or countryside. As you're walking, make sure that you turn your phone off or at least onto silent. You don't need any distractions. For that reason, it's best to do this meditation alone.

- Keep your walking pace slow, and pick out one thing about the environment you're in. It could be a tree, the clouds in the sky, a dog running around the field, anything you want to focus on
- When you're ready, zone your attention in on that item and pick out the small details. For instance, the shape of the trunk of the tree, the way the wind blows through the leaves, how the branches sway a little, etc. The idea is to notice everything about the item and keep your attention on it
- One detail should lead to another, for instance, the shape of the trunk will also cause you to think about how it extends down into the earth and how it stands majestically
- Stick with the item for five minutes at first, but as you gain more practice in this exercise, try and move up to ten minutes
- Then, choose another item and repeat the process, until your walk is finished.

Gratitude Diary

Along with journaling, you could also keep a gratitude diary. Practicing gratitude is very important for a Heyoka. At times you may feel frustrated or even bitter about your gift. It takes up so much of your time and causes you to feel a certain way a lot of the time. It's normal to feel annoyed about it sometimes. But, it's also something to be grateful for.

When you adopt a grateful mindset, you find it easier to see the positives in life, rather than the negatives. That doesn't mean you'll never become annoyed by anything or wish things were different, but you will be grateful for the positives as the first port of call.

All you need to do is write down one or two things you're grateful for out of every single day. It can be anything from enjoying a coffee with your friend to hitting a major target at work. It doesn't matter what it is, you just need to feel grateful for it. You can use your regular journal, or you can have a specific gratitude diary that you use only for this purpose. Again, avoid using apps or typing, it's best to write things down yourself.

Visualize Pushing Negative Emotions Away

When you feel like you're surrounded by negative emotions, visualization is a good way to protect yourself from their build-up. You can use visualization in any area of your life. You can also try using it to manifest good fortune and abundance your way as you become more au fait with how to use it.

The fact that you're a Heyoka means that you're already quite spiritual so visualization should come quite easily to you. However, that doesn't mean it will be automatic the first time you try it. It's very normal for your mind to wander a little, especially if you're struggling with several emotions coming your way. Stick with it and keep trying, eventually, you'll learn how to calm your mind and focus on the task at hand.

Here is a visualization exercise to try when you're struggling with an abundance of negativity.

- Go somewhere quiet and where you're not going to be distracted. This exercise will work best if you're outdoors too
- Close your eyes and turn your attention to your breath - take a deep breath in through your nose for a slow count of five, pause for a second and then exhale through your mouth for a slow count of five. Repeat as many times as you need to feel calm and grounded

- With your eyes still closed, picture the emotion(s) you want to get rid of. It might help to visualize them as a swirling ball of black, to denote negativity
- Focus on the ball and picture it in your hands, holding it far away from yourself
- Then, when you're ready, visualize yourself pushing that black ball of negativity as far away from you as you possibly can. As you do this, forcefully say or shout "no!"
- Visualize the ball flying far, far away from you, far into the distance, and disappearing past the horizon. Keep your "vision" on it until it disappears from sight
- As you do so, notice the negativity leaving your body and a sense of lightness returning
- Go back to the breathing exercise we mentioned at the start and repeat it until you feel ready to return to the moment.

Try Simple Meditation Exercises

As an empath, you're already quite spiritual, so you have a head start on learning how to meditate. However, the fact that you find it hard to concentrate may cause you problems at first. This is something you can overcome, and you'll simply need to practice in order to do that. However, meditation is something you can use to help ground you and avoid feeling overwhelmed with negativity.

There are countless meditation exercises you can try. They range from the simple to the advanced, but it's important that you don't try to run before you can walk. Don't expect to master meditation on the first few attempts, but know that with perseverance, you'll get there.

Let's take a look at two very simple meditation exercises you can start with, to show you how easy and beneficial they can be.

Body Scan Meditation

The body scan meditation exercise is a great choice for anyone who is feeling stressed, anxious, or generally achy and tired. As a Heyoka, you may notice that you manifest emotional exhaustion physically too, so it's important to be aware of how your body feels. This exercise will do that while also helping you to relax.

It goes without saying that for any meditation exercise you'll need time alone, somewhere you're not going to be distracted, without your phone or anything else that's going to cause you to snap out of your meditation without warning. You also need to be comfortable, so you'll need loose-fitting clothes and perhaps pillows and blankets to help you feel cozy.

- Lay down and make yourself comfortable
- Close your eyes and turn your attention to your breath, noticing the rise and fall of your abdomen
- When you're ready, keeping your eyes closed throughout, turn your attention now to your toes. Scrunch your toes up for a few seconds and release, noticing how they feel when you release the tension and relax. Really scan your toes for a few seconds, noticing any aches or pains
- When you're happy with your toes, move your attention up a little to your feet and tense those up, doing the same thing once more
- Repeat with your ankles, rolling them and tensing them
- Move up your legs, to your knees, to your thighs, and all the way up your body, until you reach the very top, remembering to include your arms and hands
- By the end, you should be feeling quite relaxed after tensing your muscles and then relaxing, but you should also be very aware of your body and how it feels physically
- If you notice your mind starts to wander at any point, simply return to your breath and allow thoughts to flow in and out, without paying them any attention

- When you're ready to end your meditation, tell yourself that your meditation is now over and you're going to open your eyes
- Slowly open your eyes and remain laid down for a few seconds, before slowly sitting up.

Energy Grounding Meditation

Empaths of all kinds need to learn how to ground their energy so that they're not attacked by negative forces. As a Heyoka empath, this is even more important for you to learn how to do and to practice regularly. The more grounded you are, the stronger you'll feel and the less likely it will be for you to become emotionally overwhelmed or exhausted.

- Stand with both feet flat on the floor, around a shoulder-width apart
- Close your eyes and focus on your breath, until your mind feels calm
- When you're ready, you're going to move into the mountain yoga pose. Keep your feet flat, start with your arms by your side, with your palms facing outwards. Move your shoulders, up, back, and round, so you're standing tall and powerful
- Breathe and feel your feet planted down into the ground, like a powerful tree with its roots extending below the earth
- Feel strong in your pose and feel the positive energy flowing through your body
- Every time you breathe out, feel the roots below your feet extending down, grounding you further.

White Light Protection

This is another very useful protection strategy to help you in the battle against negative energies that may come your way. If you start to feel overwhelmed or a particular emotion is very strong and you need help to deal with it, the white light protection strategy is a good one to use.

This strategy includes visualization. As with our earlier visualization of pushing a black ball of negativity away from you, this exercise includes picturing a white bubble of light around you, protecting you from anything which comes your way. Any negativity simply bounces off the bubble and cannot enter your protective shield.

Try this.

- When you feel like negativity is overwhelming you or you simply need to shield yourself from an emotion, close your eyes and focus on your breath for a few seconds until your mind calms
- Then, picture a large white bubble of light around you. It should extend down to the ground, under your feet, over your head, and all around you by around one meter
- Notice how the bubble glistens and sparkles, and any attempted negativity simply bounces off the shield
- Feel calm and protected inside the bubble and notice how you feel once you're inside
- When the feeling of being overwhelmed subsides, you can take a few breaths and return back to the moment but know that you can go back inside the bubble/shield whenever you need to. Call upon it whenever you feel upset, overwhelmed, or whenever you need a break.

Question Whether the Emotion is Yours or Someone Else's

This is a simple exercise you can use to help you identify your own emotions versus those of other people. As you become more used to being around more people, you'll find this exercise very useful.

You can use this questioning technique alongside your protective bubble/shield of white light and visualization pushing the emotion away if it doesn't belong to you.

Whenever you feel something, ask yourself "what is this emotion?" Then, put a label on it, such as anger, sadness, jealousy, etc. Then ask, "is this emotion mine?" If it's yours, that's fine, you need to deal with it in the usual way. If you cannot think of a reason why it belongs to you, put up your shield and visualize yourself pushing the emotion away from you.

As with all these protection techniques, it will get a lot easier, the more you do it.

Meditation - Protection from The Jaguar

As you become more practiced in meditation, you could use the Jaguar protection meditation exercise. This is very useful for Heyoka empaths. The jaguar is powerful and will protect you from anything. Whenever you feel you need a powerful shield, you can ask the jaguar to help you. They are known to be patient and fierce, keeping toxic energies away from you and helping you to avoid soaking them up too much.

To do this, you need to get yourself into a state of meditation. Again, this takes time to practice. All you need to do is make yourself comfortable, close your eyes and focus on your breath for as long as it takes for your mind to be completely calm. There may still be thoughts flitting in and out and that's fine, just pay them no attention. There is a false idea that to meditate you have to clear your mind of any noise, and that's not the case. It takes years of meditation practice to reach that level of proficiency.

Once you're as calm as you're able to get, call out to the jaguar spirit. Keep focusing on your breathing and notice how you feel instantly calmer when the spirit enters your space. Picture the

84

jaguar in your mind and notice how it stalks around you in a protective stance, keeping danger away from you. Feel protected and safe in its presence. Go into as much detail as you can when picturing this graceful animal and see how its face softens when it looks at you but hardens when it pictures a threat or negativity. The jaguar is there to protect you and will do you no harm.

Once you feel calmer and ready to exit your meditation, thank the jaguar and know that if you need to call on it again, you can do so.

Protect Your Work and Home Space

Sharing a space with other people can be difficult for an empath, so it's important to know how to protect your personal space as much as possible. Anything natural, such as plants, water features, crystals, and pebbles from outdoors are great things to have around your space. If you can, create a line between you and everyone else - you don't have to be obvious about this, you can just have a few plants arranged in a haphazard line that gives you a space of protection. They don't necessarily have to see it as a protective line.

If you're particularly sensitive to noise, you can also try wearing noise-canceling headphones while you're going about your day. These are far more commonplace these days, so you certainly won't stand out for wearing them.

Cleansing Yourself of Rogue Energies

At the end of every day, it's important to cleanse yourself of the energies that do not belong to you. You can do this in several different ways, and you'll find one that suits you best. Some empaths like to try sage smudging, others like to burn incense to cleanse their energies, but you can simply stick to natural methods involving water too.

Salt baths, using actual salt or Epsom salts are a good option. Water is natural and healing which means you're allowing yourself a chance to relax and cleanse at the same time. You should also make sure that you drink plenty of water throughout the day as that will help to cleanse you of energy consistently. Also, be sure to wash your hands regularly as you're literally cleansing the energies of those who have touched you.

These are several ways you can learn how to protect yourself from strong, negative energies as an empath. However, you'll also need to allow some of those in to be able to identify who you can help with your Heyoka gift. Cleansing is the single best way to rid yourself of any excess emotions at the end of every single day. If you don't do this, you'll allow a build-up and that's when you'll start to see the signs of emotional burnout heading your way.

Be mindful of protection and if something feels too strong or too much for you, use your shield and don't feel like you have to deal with it, just because you're a Heyoka. Yes, you were given this gift for a reason, but that doesn't mean you have to feel every single thing you don't want to feel. As we've said several times already, you need to look after yourself first and foremost, otherwise, you can't help anyone else.

Manage Your Gift Effectively

Looking after yourself, learning how to relax, knowing how to protect yourself, and making sure that you cleanse your energies are all key elements in living a healthy and happy life as a Heyoka empath, but you also need to know how to manage your gift.

Protection is a big part of this, but there are three other subjects that we need to cover. Your life as a Heyoka will be very rewarding, but it will also be a little chaotic if you don't learn how to manage your gift and focus on the positives.

Here are three other subsections you need to know about when it comes to side-stepping problems and managing your rather remarkable gift as a Heyoka empath.

Always Set Strong Boundaries

When you set boundaries, you're not pushing people out or refusing to help, you're looking after your own health and wellbeing. This is vital as an empath of any type, but as a Heyoka, it's even more important.

This particular point relates to boundaries with your physical environment and your ability to say "yes" or "no" to people. As a Heyoka, you soak up energies very easily and that means that your home needs to be a place of sanctuary. If you live alone, this point is a little easier than if you live with someone else.

You need to have a space in your home that is yours and yours alone. Nobody should touch anything in that space (because they will transfer their energy to it), and they should respect your need for privacy and space. You're not being rude or pushing anyone out; remember that this space and these boundaries are important for your emotional and physical health.

It's very easy for people to take advantage of you because you're so caring and sensitive but you also need to be very firm when you do not want to do something. Don't feel like you have to agree to everything - you don't. Learn to say "no" when you want to say it and feel okay with it. Do not allow guilt to overwhelm you - there's no need for you to feel that way.

Communicate as Much as You Can

For some empaths, when they first realize their gift, they're quite shy about talking about it. It's true that many people simply don't understand. We don't tend to believe anything we can't see or measure, but it's important that you talk to your nearest and dearest about your Heyoka nature.

You can't expect them to understand your quirks or your boundaries if you don't explain why you need them. You shouldn't have to convince them - if you find that you're doing that then simply put forward your explanation and leave it with them. But, they should respect what you're saying. Know that they're not mind-readers, they can't read other people as well as you do! So, you'll need to talk.

If you're feeling overwhelmed, talk to your partner, your parents, your friend, anyone who is very close to you. Let them know when you need a little space, so they don't feel like they've done something wrong.

If you're struggling, open up. Bottling up emotions is not going to help you; it doesn't help anyone, and it certainly does nothing for a Heyoka.

This is particularly important if you're in a relationship with someone. It may be that at times you need to withdraw and ground yourself. Talk to your partner about this. It might also be that you simply don't want to be touched at times. Rather than just pulling away and leaving them feeling confused, be sure to explain why and open up.

Relationships are difficult for Heyokas, in fact, they're difficult for any empath, but they're not impossible. Communicating is extremely important. Without it, you'll find that misunderstandings run amok, and your relationships don't last for more than a few months at best.

Learning to Trust Your Intuition

As a Heyoka empath, your intuition is very strong. At times you might be taken aback by how strong it is. As you're learning about your gift, or when you're first realizing that you have it, you might struggle with knowing when it's your intuition speaking and when it's paranoia or something else entirely.

This is normal. Everyone struggles with listening to their inner voice occasionally but yours is shouting at you - literally screaming. It's important that you listen to it, but even more importantly, you have to trust it. Your intuition is going to be your guide throughout your empathic life. Consider it the best friend that will never steer you wrong.

The chances are that if you think back, there will be many situations in your life so far when your intuition has guided you to the right outcome. But, if you're struggling with intuitive trust, here are a few tips you can use to build that trust and finally learn to rely upon your gut to help you through your empathic life.

- **Take time to be calm and still** - On a regular basis, you need to be calm and still as an empath anyway, but when it comes to following your intuition, you need to quiet your mind to actually listen to it. This is where meditation can help.
- **Practice mindfulness** - We talked about mindfulness a little earlier and this is a great strategy for helping you to feel more trusting of your intuition. Being in the moment means that you're not always thinking back to the past or forward to the future. You're firmly grounded in the now.
- **Deliberately tune into your intuition** - Sit down, close your eyes, focus on your breath, and then ask your inner voice what it's trying to tell you. Be patient. At first, you might not get anything, or you might feel like you're getting several different answers all at once. Stick with it. Once you get a

message or a feeling like you're supposed to do a certain thing or advice to say something, write it down. You'll probably find that it guides you at some point in the very near future.

- **Ask your intuition to help you** - As with tuning into your intuition, a good way to learn how to trust it is to use it. Ask your intuition to help you with a problem or a quandary you're facing. Then, tune into it and see what the message is. You have a very strong intuition as a Heyoka empath, but the more you use it, the stronger it will be.
- **Follow your inner voice** - Even if you're not sure, go with what your gut is telling you. Just like working out at the gym builds your muscles, using your intuition builds its strength. Again, the more you use it, the more you can rely upon it. So, when you feel like it's telling you something, go with it and see how often it is right.
- **Keep your mind open** - As a Heyoka empath, you have a very open-minded approach to life anyway. But when things start to become tough or you're unsure of your gift, it's normal to close up a little. Don't allow that to happen. Make sure that you maintain an open mind and don't judge.
- **Look for any synchronicities in your day** - As you're using your intuition, be sure to look for coincidences or synchronicities as you go about your day. It's a good idea to scribble these down as they probably won't make much sense in the moment. But, when you piece them together with what your gut is telling you, you'll see the bigger picture. Writing them down will also give you the proof you need that your intuition is guiding you, even if you can't bring yourself to fully trust it just yet.

As a Heyoka empath, your intuition is your guide. As you notice disturbances in the energy around you, you'll also notice that your inner voice kicks into gear too. You have to listen to it and allow it to become your own best friend.

Points to Remember

This chapter has been a bumper one! As we mentioned at the start, it's a good idea to scribble down notes of any strategies that really jump out at you. It could be your intuition guiding you toward something that it knows is going to work for you. But, trying several strategies for protecting yourself as a Heyoka empath is a good idea.

You're always surrounded by negativity of some kind but, believe it or not, you have a choice as to how much it affects you. You can learn how to manage your gift and protect yourself from too much negativity. This is a must-do for any empath. As a Heyoka, it's even more important. Without doing so, you run the risk of approaching burnout or emotional exhaustion. This can lead to illness and depression over the long term.

In this chapter we've talked at length about how to protect yourself and why it's important to find calmness and serenity regularly. It's not selfish to want to spend time alone and to focus on yourself, it's a true necessity. By doing this, setting boundaries, communicating, and learning a few meditation and cleansing routines, you'll find that your life as a Heyoka is fulfilling, rather than constantly making you feel stressed and burnt out.

Chapter 6:
How To Improve Lives with Your Empathic Gift

We're onto our final chapter! How do you feel now? Hopefully, you're feeling uplifted and positive about the world of the Heyoka empath and fascinated to learn even more.

Being a sponge for emotions can indeed be difficult but it's also such a wonderful thing to have in your life and a fascinating subject. In this final chapter, we want to end on a truly positive note. In our last chapter, we talked a lot about how to make life easier for you and how to manage your gift. That has to be done because we can't deny that life for a Heyoka can be hard sometimes. But, and this is a big 'but', you have the most wonderful gift within you.

We're going to talk in this last section about how you can enrich your life with your gift and how you can use it to turn around the lives of those around you. You can even try to develop your empathic gifts and push things a little further if you choose to - maybe you want to see just how powerful you can really be!

Being a Heyoka Can Improve Your Life

In our earlier pros and cons section, we talked about how being a Heyoka empath can help you to become more confident and to have a large amount of self-worth. That's a huge plus point and in terms of how being a Heyoka can improve your life, that's seriously up there towards the top of the list.

But, how else can your Heyoka gift actually improve your life?

How about that wonderful sense of doing good for other people? That's a major starting point. It helps you to feel calm and happy within yourself. Sometimes we all doubt ourselves and wonder whether we're good people and whether we're truly doing the best we can for ourselves and others. But, as a Heyoka, you're going above and beyond. You've been asked to do a lot and you're smashing it every single time. You should be proud of what you're doing and even if you're struggling a little at times, know that you're doing your best and that's more than good enough.

Another way in which your Heyoka gift can help improve your life is that you have an internal compass within you that will never serve you wrong. We talked about how to increase your trust in your intuition earlier and that's something you should certainly pay some attention to. Your intuition will be the one thing that will never let you down. It will never be wrong. Even if you don't like what it is telling you, it's not wrong.

Many people struggle with decisions and that's something you have a problem with occasionally too. But, by tapping into your intuition and understanding that it is there for a positive reason, you'll always feel confident in your ability to never put a foot wrong. And, even if you do make a wrong turn occasionally, know that you probably had to make that mistake to learn and grow.

As a Heyoka, you're completely at one with nature and in tune with the energies around you. While having relationships and friendships can be difficult from time to time, you can learn to set boundaries and create loving and close unions. When that happens, you'll be able to grow closer than "regular" couples. You can feel what they're feeling and as long as you're open and able to communicate effectively with them, they'll feel that sense of true closeness to you too.

Put simply, life as a Heyoka is an adventure. And, what could be better than that?

Being a Heyoka Can Improve the Lives of Others

Of course, the most obvious thing to talk about is that you're able to help people to move away from situations that are causing them to hurt or something that harms them. You're able to heal people by allowing them to explore their behaviors and problems. You're empowering them with the ability to choose to change their lives. You're not telling them what to do, you're encouraging them to explore and reflecting everything back to them in a way that guides them towards the right conclusion.

Let's consider this for a second. As a Heyoka empath, you could save someone's life. It's really that special. You may come across someone who is struggling with a lot of negativity and darkness, and they don't know which way to turn. While absorbing that amount of negativity will be hard for you, there are protective methods you can use to shield yourself. But, within that, you have the extreme power to help them to heal. You can help them to turn their lives around. You're giving them the confidence and the push to do something good and move away from the darkness.

How amazing would that feel for both you and them?

At times, your gift may feel like a curse. But, those moments will be fleeting and they won't last for long. As you see the effect you're having on people and the positivity you're bringing into their lives, you'll be determined to keep on doing more of the same.

You're a true gift to the world with your ability and that's something you should hold close to your heart at all times. It may not always come easily but repeat after us - "I am special. I don't need to be like anyone else. I am me". Go on, shout it from the rooftops!

How To Increase Your Empathic Ability

Before we leave you, we want to help you to push your abilities even further. You already have the strength and tremendous power within you, but what if you could push that to another level? What if you could develop your Heyoka gift to be a true superpower?

Well, you can. It takes time and effort, but you can develop your empathic ability and keep building your confidence at the same time. The methods to develop your gift are quite easy to start with, but you will need to practice them regularly to build up to a noticeable improvement.

But, it's important to know that you already have everything you need inside of you. There are no "regular" Heyokas and "super" Heyokas. A Heyoka is powerful enough no matter what. The only thing you can do to develop your power is to know what grounds you, to understand how to look after yourself, and to trust what you're feeling. Those are the best ways to develop and push your gifts towards something truly earth-shattering - in the very best way, of course.

Let's take a look at a few ways you can increase and build upon your Heyoka empathic ability.

Acknowledge Your Gift Every Day

You will not enter into your true power until you acknowledge and make peace with your nature. You are a wonderful and powerful being and you need to be happy with your Heyoka gift. It may feel difficult at first, but by following the advice in this book you'll see that your nature is a truly positive thing. Then, you can learn to accept your gift and it will grow from there.

Without acknowledgement, you'll always be struggling with self-doubt and lacking trust in your intuition. When you step into your power, it's because you've said, "this is me, I am a Heyoka empath, and I am here to heal". If you want to, you can use it as a positive mantra that you repeat daily!

Of course, if you fail to acknowledge your gift and you try to push it aside, it won't go anywhere. You can't turn this off like a switch. You'll always feel the way you do, but you won't know how to handle it. That's not something you need in your life. Your gift is entirely manageable. Acknowledge it, learn about it, and embrace it. It's the best way forward and in truth, the only way forward.

Avoid Playing the Victim Card

When you're close to emotional exhaustion, it's possible that you are so full of negativity that you're struggling with your self-worth. The key to developing your gift is knowing when this is happening and stepping away from the situation. You're not a victim. you're the one with the power in their hands and you could never be described as a victim of any sort.

Playing the victim often looks a lot like the symptoms of approaching burnout. We talked about those earlier on, so if you do notice that you're starting to feel quite pessimistic, you're avoiding the things you normally enjoy, and you're wallowing in what can only be described as self-pity, it's time to drag yourself out of it. Be kind to yourself, focus on your own recovery, and spend some time in nature.

Playing the victim doesn't help you and it certainly won't endear you to anyone else either.

Identify Energy Vampires

If you want to build on your gift, you need to stop those around you who are trying to zap your energy away. These are known as 'energy vampires' and they're the people who make you feel exhausted or extremely negative, simply by standing next to them. You'll know who they are simply by questioning how you feel and where it is coming from. Then, if you notice a pattern, it's because this person is draining the positive light out of you.

As a Heyoka, you need to identify energy vampires and steer clear of them as much as possible. Use your white light shield when they're in your vicinity and your gift will remain strong and powerful.

As a quick note, there is one particular type of person who is a threat to any empath, Heyoka or not. The narcissist.

The narcissist and the empath are a match made in a literal hell. There will be no pleasant outcome when a narcissist sets their sights on an empath and the empath tries to forgive the narcissist's manipulation over and over. You might assume that your strong intuition and ability to spot liars will protect you from this type of manipulation, but we're sorry to say that it won't completely.

The reason? Your heart.

Empaths are wonderfully pure and beautiful souls. You don't want to believe that someone could be that cruel or that negative. So, you try to look past the things they say and do, trying to look for the good amongst the bad. The issue is, there isn't much good there.

Now, we should point out that true narcissists do have a personality disorder. It isn't their fault, per se. But their actions and their cruelty do not mean you should forgive them. Narcissistic Personality Disorder is characterized by a very low amount of empathy and in most cases, a total lack. Narcissists cannot love you. They can't love anyone. They don't even love themselves. As a Heyoka, you might want to try and use your special healing skills to try and help them but trust us when we say that it won't work. They have a disorder that will not be changed through careful thinking or soul searching. You cannot love them into changing because they simply can't change.

Narcissists have a habit of seeking out empaths because of their kind nature. That makes them open to manipulation. Yes, that sounds quite a negative thing for us to say, but your heart is so open that they can see straight into it.

For your own sake, do not allow that darkness into your heart. If you spot a narcissist, or you're even on the fence about whether someone in your life falls into that category, wish them well, and walk away from them. Say goodbye with love in your heart and let it go.

It will not end well if you stay. If you think emotional exhaustion sounds bad, that's nothing compared to the aftermath of narcissistic abuse.

Keep Refreshing and Resetting Boundaries

You already know that to manage your gift, you need to set boundaries. But, to develop your skills you need to regularly question whether the boundaries are working and whether you need to reset them and adjust what you already have in place. Be aware of how you feel in specific situations and use your journal to identify patterns. If you feel that something isn't working for you, have the strength to set a boundary that helps you to feel in control. By doing this, your power will grow because the amount of negativity you attract will lessen.

You'll also feel much more at peace in your life when you have strong boundaries in place. Again, never feel guilty or upset about setting a boundary. If someone cares about you, they will understand. It's also true that situations change regularly, so it could be that a boundary you set a while ago just isn't working as well as it could anymore. You will need to review it and change it to help you to feel more in control and calmer nowadays.

Reduce Negative Energy Build up With Transmutation

We know that as a Heyoka, you absorb a lot of negative energy and we've talked about many strategies you can use to protect yourself, but transmutation is something you can try too. This will rid you of negative energy build-up and clear the way for you to focus on listening to your intuition and developing your gift through regular use.

The good news is that transmutation isn't nearly as difficult as the term makes it sound! Here are a few ways you can kick out (transmute) negativity:

- Incorporate plants into your life as much as possible
- Keep crystals in your pocket to help balance your energies - Focus on different crystals and choose the one that really stands out to you. There are countless different crystals, and they all have specific uses. But, the crystal chooses you, not the other way around. By looking carefully at a set of crystals and noticing which one really stands out to you, you'll find the one that will protect you the most. But, you'll need to cleanse your crystal regularly, just as you need to cleanse yourself. You and the crystal are not that different from one another!
- Do more of the things you love!
- Reframe your words and thoughts from negativity to positivity and do so mindfully
- Look for humor wherever possible, but never at the expense of someone else
- Use positive affirmations daily
- Practice gratitude

- Use the body scan meditation (mentioned earlier) to help scan your body and heal from any aches and pains caused by a negativity build-up

These methods will help you to shed negativity away from you and focus on accepting positivity into your heart. If you start to feel subdued and weighed down, recognize the signs of build-up and start pushing it away. But, it's best to practice these methods daily before you get to that point so that you can keep negativity levels as low as possible.

Meditate Daily

We've already mentioned that meditation is a good idea for Heyoka empaths, because of their spiritual connections. But, if you want to develop your gift, it's a good idea to meditate daily. If possible, up to three times a day.

Meditation will help you to remain calm and grounded, but it will also help to develop your connection with your higher self. Meditation can also help you to avoid overload, especially when you feel like all your senses are full to the brim.

If sitting down and meditating is difficult for you because of time constraints, either change your schedule a little or simply head outdoors and seek out a quiet and tranquil spot within nature. Using your white light shield is also a meditation of sorts. Practice as much as possible and you'll find that your gift strengthens, as well as your confidence and wellbeing.

Use Your Gift as Much as You Can

The best way to develop your ability is to use it! The more you use your intuition, the more you'll trust it. The more you use your empathic gift, the more you'll embrace it and be able to help others around you.

If you don't enjoy your gift, it's easy to try and push it down, but that won't work. You'll still absorb negativity, but you won't know what to do with it. You'll still feel overwhelmed, in fact, you'll feel even more overwhelmed, and you'll be unsure of the techniques to reduce it. Life will be much better and far more fulfilling if you embrace the gift you have, learn how to use it, and use it as much as you can.

While you can't develop your Heyoka gift into something akin to Superman, you can focus on developing it through self-improvement. You can look to keep yourself grounded and positive, pushing away negativity and understanding that your nature is something to be proud of. When you do that, you'll notice that your ability to understand and read people grows naturally.

The difference between an empath who has fully embraced and accepted their gift and an empath who refuses to accept it or simply has no idea what is going on is huge. Life gets easier when you embrace and accept. It's really that simple. Then, the only way is up because you have all the information in this book to put to good use!

Love Yourself As Well As Your Gift

Developing your gift isn't about going to school and learning anything. The single best ways to learn how to develop your Heyoka abilities are to focus on how you feel and what you do on a day-to-day basis. Within all of this, you need to learn to love yourself and be grateful for the gift you've been given.

Remember that looking after yourself is one of your main priorities in life. This isn't a selfish act, it's something that is part of your gift. It's one of the things you need to do in order to function. Every single day, set some time aside to sit down and look at how you're feeling. Tell yourself that you're wonderful and actually mean it! Honor the emotions that are running through you and take note of any sensitive points, releasing negativity and filling yourself with love.

Points to Remember

How do you feel at the end of this last chapter? I hope that you're brimming with Hope and Positivity!

We've talked in this chapter about how your empathic ability as a Heyoka is a gift. It's something that was given to you because you are a sensitive and intuitive individual. You're someone with the power to heal and change the lives of those around them. Yes, at times you feel overwhelmed, but there is plenty for you to do to reduce that and to understand how to manage your nature.

It's not just the people around you who benefit from your Heyoka gifts, you benefit too. Your deep love and respect for who you are and the satisfaction you gain from helping others will be something you can't even put into words. We can't even put it into words! You'll also have a strong and reliable guide in your intuition, always there for you whenever you need a helping hand.

We've also talked about how you can learn how to develop your gift by using it as much as possible and looking after yourself. The truth is that you already have everything you need inside of you, you simply need to put the pieces together and find your way.

Conclusion

Congratulations on reaching the end of the book and learning about the wonderful and fascinating world of the Heyoka empath. By this point, you're sure to have a world of insight into this powerful type of empath and you might be keen to start developing your own empathic gifts too. Keep going!

The fact that you have reached the end of this book shows that you're someone who doesn't give up easily. Only 10% of people who read a book get to the end. So, you're special already, because you're someone who is able to finish what they started. You had the determination and focus to dedicate yourself to learning and that should be congratulated.

Of course, the fact that you read this far means that you enjoyed what you read, but it also means that you found the content useful. That makes us extremely happy. The reason this book was written was to help people like you. Now you can go forth and put what you've learned to good use! You'll help yourself and those around you by doing this.

What you have learned has the power to change your life and the lives of other people. But now, you have to put into practice what you've learned and embrace it fully. Cast any doubts aside and believe in the power of the empath. Discovery and learning are only 10% information. You can read about anything and know a few facts, but is that true learning? No! Real learning is absorbing and exploring. Putting things into practice and finding out what works for you. It's true when they say that learning is 90% practice, and your practice time starts right now!

You have all the information you need, but the final brick in the wall is confidence. Do you have the confidence to take what you've learned and run with it? If not, why not? In fact, if not, go back and read it again!

Anything is possible, the Heyoka empathic world teaches us that very fact.

Being a Heyoka is a Life's Calling

You might be wondering who is chosen to be a Heyoka and who isn't. And, whether we can develop the life of a Heyoka if we aren't born with the gift. The truth is, you're born a   Heyoka. You're born with that special seed inside of you. As you grow, it grows with you. But, in order to develop fully, you have to embrace your gift and learn to manage it.

Do you feel that you're a Heyoka empath? Or, maybe you feel like you're a different type of empath? Maybe you've read this book and decided that you're not an empath but that you're someone who is highly sensitive, and you can benefit from many of the relaxation and protection strategies we've talked about throughout the book.

It might also be that you've identified someone in your life who has the Heyoka gift. Maybe they don't know it yet, and they're struggling with understanding why they feel the way they do. You have the chance to show them the way forward and help them to understand what is going on and how to embrace it.

They say that knowledge is power and, in this case, that couldn't be more true.

Maintaining a positive mindset is the single best way to banish negativity. Visualize a cloud of darkness being pushed away and broken up into tiny pieces by the shining, white light of positivity. That's how powerful it can be. Time and time again we've seen examples of the power of positivity throughout humanity and there's no reason why it can't do the very same thing for you.

Let's Sum Up

We're about to let go of the grip we've had on your hand for the last six chapters and watch you go out into the big, wide world with your new confidence in place. But before we do that, let's sum up the main points of what we've learned together.

The Heyoka empath is the most powerful type of empath. As a Heyoka, you have an extreme amount of empathy and intuition, and you're able to act as a mirror to help people in need explore their problems and look toward different perspectives and ways to solve them. You often do this with humor, and you have a knack for knowing exactly the right thing to say, at the right time. You can also read people very well, and you can spot a liar from very far away.

Of course, there are many other types of empaths out there, but the Heyoka is considered the most powerful because of their special ability to heal with a mirror and humor. No other type of empath can heal in this way. So, if you're truly a Heyoka, you're the most special of them all!

We've talked a lot about how to manage your gift and really tried to push home the fact that although life as a Heyoka can be difficult at the time, it is a gift that was given to you for a reason. You're strong enough to handle it otherwise it wouldn't be in your possession. You've also been chosen to help others in this way because of the huge amount of kindness and empath you have in your heart. You're a truly wonderful and gentle soul, someone who can change the world in the best way possible.

By protecting yourself from a build-up of negative energy, you can go about your daily business just as anyone else would. You're not constantly bombarded with people who need your help - this is something that happens ad hoc. You can have relationships, as long as you set boundaries and make sure that you communicate effectively. You can choose a job that suits your creative tendencies and really have a true sense of job satisfaction from it. You can also take great pride in the people that you do help, even if you're not totally aware that you're helping them at the time!

The main point to take away is that your gift isn't a burden. It's not something that you can't handle. It's just something that you need to learn about first. You can't be expected to know how to handle your empathic nature if you're not aware of what is happening and why you're feeling the way you are. You need knowledge and that's what this book has aimed to give you. Again, it may be that you're not an empath, but you can tell someone around you is. In that case, help them to explore their gift by explaining what you've learned and passing the book onto them.

Negativity will not overwhelm you if you know how to protect yourself. Your gift can't harm you when you understand it and know how to counteract the negativity you may encounter from those around you. And while you may get tired occasionally, it's the best type of tired because you know that you're feeling that way out of helping other people. You don't have to be totally selfless, because you're human first and empath second. But, you do need to have the right mindset to be able to fully appreciate and enjoy the empath lifestyle.

Because yes, you really can enjoy it! Trust us, it's entirely within reach. And who knows, maybe by learning about your gift you'll meet other empaths in your local area and you can learn more together.

One Last Thing Before You Go …

Before we bid you goodbye, we have a quick favor to ask. It's only small and it won't take long.

We want to reach out to as many people and help them in the same way we've helped you, but we can only do that if people comment and review our book. That way, we can be noticed by far more! A huge 91% of readers look toward reviews before they buy a book. Perhaps you did that before you chose this book? Honest reviews are important for authors, and they help us to continue doing what we love best.

So, if you feel that this book helped you and that it gave you a sense of purpose and positivity, we would be very grateful if you could take just a few seconds of your time to leave us a review. Let us know what you think! We'd love to know what you enjoyed, what you found helpful, and what you'd like to learn more about. And don't worry about us reading it - we read every single one. Reviews are an incomparable source of feedback and motivation.

Here's how you can give us your feedback:

- If you're enjoying this book on audible, hit the three dots in the top right of your device. Then click 'rate and review' and leave us a few sentences about the book, finishing with a star rating.
- If you're reading on an e-reader or Kindle, you can simply scroll to the bottom of the book and then swipe up. You'll automatically be taken to a screen that prompts you to leave a review.
- If the above points don't work (functionality changes all the time), you can simply go to the page you purchased this book, such as Amazon, and leave a review directly on the page.

Your reviews and honest feedback really do mean the world and will allow us to keep helping people around the world.

Now, all that's left to say is goodbye and good luck. Good luck on your empath journey and your development as a powerful and formidable Heyoka. You have the power to change the world for so many people. Now go forth and harness that power!

THE INTUITIVE EMPATH SELF CARE GUIDE AGAINST
GASLIGHTING, NARCISSISTIC ABUSE & ENERGY VAMPIRES

DARK EMPATH

SET BOUNDARIES, GUARD YOURSELF AGAINST
NEGATIVE ENERGY, STOP CODEPENDENT
TOXIC RELATIONSHIPS

SOPHIA SWANN

SUMMARY

Introduction

Dear reader, I want to extend my congratulations on starting or continuing your journey as an empath. The path of an empath can be lonely, overwhelming, or feel wildly unanchoring. You may be doing your best in doing your self-work, structuring your path, and learning how to hone your skills. There are others, however, who will create obstacles for you. There are people who will disrupt your journey in often emotionally distressing and psychologically draining ways. We call these people "dark empaths", "energy vampires", and/or narcissists. They all have rather flexible meanings and classifications, but the general trait in common is that all of these types of people can be obstacles, learning opportunities, and reminders to protect ourselves.

You have probably met a dark empath before. A dark empath is not possessed by a malignant spirit. They are often not even a "bad" person. Some can have ill intentions, like abusers and narcissists. Other dark empaths are more or less other empaths that do not know how to set healthy boundaries and often cross-contaminate their own metaphysical and emotional baggage with others. Some dark empaths are more manipulative and know how to toy with the emotions of another to gain something.

Not every energy vampire is a dark empath. Many of them are folks who are out of balance with themselves. Energy vampires carry a number of identifiable traits, which will be described in detail in this book.

It is helpful to point out that it is not your responsibility to change, mentor, or guide energy vampires. Although, when there is consent, symbiotic, and healthy boundaries in place, it is possible to make a positive impact, but that should not be our goal.

Most people don't want to change. Those who do will pick up books like this one, and even amongst those consumers, less than 10%

will actually read the book. The fact that you're reading this book right now makes you amongst the top 10%. This marks a commitment and interest in your own emotional and spiritual well-being. Even if you do not consider yourself an empath, this book can reveal lessons and insight into the kind of tools you need to deal with different flavors of toxic people. Moreover, any person can find setting healthy boundaries to be a useful habit. Using this book to identify people with incompatible energies is also something that does not require associating yourself to being an empath. The contents in each chapter will empower you with knowledge, including descriptions of various dark empaths, energy vampires, and other types of folks who can be obstacles in maintaining our inner peace and balance. You will also be given tools to use to prepare yourself in times of conflict with dark empaths.

This book may seem to you like a monster-hunting guide or a way to ID problematic folks. As I said before, energy vampires and vibe-ruining individuals are not necessarily bad people. Some have just lost their way of maintaining balance. It is not your job to fix them, nor is it your obligation to let their energy into your aura to mesh with it. That is why creating boundaries and ways to protect yourself mentally, spiritually, emotionally, and physically is extremely important. Otherwise, you leave yourself vulnerable to manipulation, torment, heartbreak, burnout, and a wide variety of soul-sickening ailments.

Chapters not focused on other people will teach you how to reflect, perform self-check-ins, and be mindful of your various states of being. It is wise to know how to protect yourself from outside energies and is also important to make time for introspection and knowing yourself. The more we maintain our own vessel, our own mindset, and our own well-being, the better we are equipped to help others.

We are in this together as a community of empaths, creatives, and highly sensitive types. In the age of the internet, we are "connected" more than ever through ethernet cables, wifi connections, social media posts, and various truths and perspectives, it can be hard to feel any genuine connection.

You may read some stories about friendships or people I know. Please note that their names have been changed to maintain their privacy, but they have consented to share their story in an effort to educate.

Once you have finished this book, you will have started your transformative journey and will have a foundation, tools, boundaries, and forms of protection for your various energy fields and physical body. You can always come back to this book if you need a reminder.

In our vision to bring guides and spiritual resilience toolkits to more individuals and communities, we hope that you leave a review that will show others the usefulness and quality of this book. Your rating and approval can inspire others to stop their own self-destruction or to gain a curiosity about remembering their self-worth.

1. What is an Empath?

"Let me hold the door for you.

I may have never walked in your shoes,

but I can see: your soles are worn,

your strength is torn

under the weight of a story

I have never lived before.

Let me hold the door for you.

After all you've walked through,

It's the least I can do."

Morgan Harper Nichols

The Difference between Empathy and being an Empath

I recall reading a webcomic that explained the nature of sympathy and empathy quite well: In the cartoon, Person A is standing above, looking into a hole, and has an understanding that Person B is stuck in the hole. Person A says that they are very sorry. This is sympathy. In the next panel, a second person is looking into the hole, and then gets a rope, climbs in, and says "I know how you feel."

Empathy is described as a "vicarious, spontaneous sharing of affect, can (sic) be provoked by witnessing another's emotional state, by hearing about another's condition, or even by reading." (Keen 2006) Empathy often moves one toward compassion or altruistic action, rather than avoidance or distress.

Most people experience empathy to some degree, with some exceptions. Leading empath and empathy expert Dr. Judith Orloff defines empathy as: "...when we reach our hearts out to others and put ourselves in their shoes." (Orloff) Being an empath, however, is entirely different. Empaths often feel the emotions and energy levels of others spiritually, emotionally, physically, and mentally. This can vary from person to person. Many trained empaths can turn off a few aspects. For the empath that has no proper boundaries, coping skills, or energetic walls and filters, all of this information can be incredibly overwhelming and overstimulating.

Psychologists have identified three different types of empathy: Cognitive, emotional, and compassionate. Cognitive empathy is when a person can understand someone's perspective and thoughts (Gillette, 2022). This is more centered around their objective knowledge of the matter.

Emotional or affective empathy is when one can feel the emotions someone else is experiencing as though they are also experiencing them (Gillette, 2022). Compassionate empathy is a mix of the two, in which one understands the point of view of someone and feels the emotions of another. Compassionate empathy usually moves someone into action to help, but not so much to the point in which the lines between one's own emotions and others are blurred. This is connected to the idea of Buddhist loving-kindness. When a person makes a proactive choice in helping, they will often also experience sympathetic joy, by observing the way their selfless act has made someone's day (Derisz).

We know through observable evidence that humans learn from one another. As infants we learn from our parents' language, movement, expression, and daily actions. Babies even pick up on how we express specific emotions. One hypothesis of why this occurs is through mirror neurons.

It has been suggested in psychological and holistic health circles that we are hard-wired for empathy due to the existence of mirror neurons. Mirror neurons in our brains allow us to experience empathy. In studies, the human and monkey brains can observe behavior in others of their own species, and either imitate the behavior or process it. The same part of our brains lights up, as though we are going through the activity or behavior we are observing. In another study, it was found that observing another person's action, pain, or reaction can trigger parts of the same neural networks responsible for executing those actions and experiencing action, pain, or feeling as though they were feeling it in their own physical body (Armstrong). If we consider mirror neurons and empaths, we can probably assume that under this model, empaths would have very active mirror neurons.

The anterior cingulate cortex and anterior insula are in the salience network of human brain regions that activate in response to salient stimuli In individuals with autism, the recognition of social stimuli may be diminished in their salient area, leading to atypical social skills. Social stimuli may include such as facial microexpressions, eyes, and gaze. Empaths with anxiety are believed to have hyper-responsive mirror neurons. Psychopaths would have limited or nonexistent responses to the distress of another, often unable to feel remorse or relate to others, especially in terms of disgust, fear, or sadness. Dark empaths' mirror neurons would be active, but they would not respond to them as though they were feeling it. They would quickly assess a person in pain and then try to figure out how to exploit the emotion, or be helpful so that they can use the person later. Dark empaths may also have been good empaths at one point, but are presently able to use the data from their empathy to inform them of how to be helpful - optimizing advantages later. They numb themselves from experiencing the person's pain as well.

Two other hypotheses of how we experience empathy are embodied cognition theory and common coding theory. Common coding theory supposes that physical action, like wiggling your fingers, is represented in your brain. You need to command your hands to do things. Our brain needs to be able to convert this representative language of things we are hearing or seeing, and things that we are doing. Watching someone kick the ball, is coded in our brain as "kick the ball". Perceiving someone crying in our heads, our brain is signaling "you should be crying". If you ever have watched someone watch sports, you may have seen this behavior. A person who is watching a kickboxing match will try to swing and punch as though they are in the match too.

A different hypothesis, embodied cognition theory, is a thesis that challenges other theories. The premise is that there is the world around you. You perceive it, process it, and then act. Everything we process is translated concretely and connected to our perception of our physical body. We are incapable of processing things in the abstract. For instance, let's say you see a horror movie. You watch a person get stabbed in the eye. Your brain is not just saying "that's uncomfortable", your body is having a visceral reaction, and your eye is now probably twitching, or squinting. Perhaps your head flinched backward when you saw the stabbing.

There are now virtual reality (VR) experiences. In some scenarios, people using the technology get to experience living like refugees. Some other scenarios are about solitary confinement. The people who play these games self-reported feeling sick to their stomach and similar visceral reactions. VR is starting to get to a point where embodied cognition theory informs us that virtual experiences are enough to have an emotional and physical reaction.

In my youth, I did not believe that empathy could be weaponized to manipulate, exploit, and harm others. Empathy appeared to me as a gift to give, or a random act of kindness that you did just because. The more I lived and understood the world around me, the more I realized the world was not in black and white. Some people could appear good: philanthropists, healers, teachers, social justice leaders, social workers, and therapists, all hiding in spaces where the vulnerable are an easy target. It gives the people that exist in those spaces a bad name, especially the ones that wish to do right by their occupation or position. The ones that follow the principles and integrity of the teacher or healer are not there for glory, fame, or appreciation; they are there to do what needs to be done without hesitation or praise.

When it comes to dark empaths, their confidence and charisma can make them difficult to identify. Their seemingly genuine concern and desire to be helpful can disarm their prey. Reasonable boundaries and limits are removed or ignored under the guise of charm and attention.

Questions for Reflection:

(These will be at the end of each chapter. I encourage you to keep a journal so that you can monitor your journey and ponderings for your growth and benefit)

If you consider yourself an empath, what does it mean to you to be one?

Do you ever feel like you care too much and wish you didn't? Why?

What is your goal while reading this book?

Who is a person you can think about while reading this book? Are you worried for them, or are you hoping you can set more boundaries with them?

2. What Is A Dark Empath

A Dark Empath can hide in many forms and take many forms. They are often just as sensitive and attuned to energies emanated by humans, animals, forces, the universe, etc. The Dark Empath, however, will often misuse their gifts, sometimes much like a supervillain, or something far less nefarious. The kind of Dark Empaths that use their empathy skills know what you want and feel, and are ready to use it against you. It is helpful for you to have a toolbox for protecting yourself from Dark Empaths. Like the superstition of wearing garlic when a vampire is in the room, you will have to put up boundaries to uninvite the unwelcome energy from such people that disturb your peace.

If we recall the webcomic mentioned in the first chapter with our friend trapped in a hole, a third possible panel could have been a person attempting to pull the other up. This might indicate an empath acting compassionately, or helping without consent. What if the person wanted to stay stuck in the hole? Or what if the empath did not have the strength to pull their friend out, and fell in too? Another image could have been a person yelling at them to climb up without supplying any rope? Sounds like toxic positivity to me. What if the non-stuck person was digging their hole and also complaining about how stuck they were? What if they rescued the person in the hole and demanded payment afterward?

These new metaphors explain how being an empath without any mindfulness, healthy boundaries, or ethics can result in either some empathy burnout or some seriously toxic traits. In the chapters to come, we will be identifying Dark Empath traits and creating strategies to keep ourselves safe and sane in their presence.

Additionally, we can use different kinds of protection to filter out, or perhaps become immune to their influence.

This book will teach you how to avoid becoming a Dark Empath, as well as teach you how to protect yourself from other Dark Empaths. Being a highly sensitive person or an Empath and being aware of it, also predisposes us to meet the same fate as a Dark Empath might. Without proper practices and boundaries, no one is exempt from becoming toxic or expressing toxic traits; the best we can do is know ourselves, form good habits, and surround ourselves with a supportive community.

Psychology has entertained the notion of the Dark Empath by noting the dark triad of traits often found in Dark Empaths. The dark triad (DT) consists of Machiavellianism, psychopathy, and narcissism (Heym et al., 2021)

People can have Dark Triad traits, like narcissists and some psychopaths, without being an empath. What is interesting about Dark Empaths is how they are known to have high empathy, but still carry the DT traits. This is thought to make them more dangerous than people with DT traits alone because dark empaths tend to be emotional shapeshifters. Dark Empaths tend to be less aggressive than those with DT traits only; this makes it easier for dark empaths to go undetected and chameleon their way through situations. Their expertise in social skills and relatability makes them very unlike a psychopath or sociopath. Because of their DT traits, they do not feel remorse or shame for exploiting their knowledge of subtle behaviors and emotions.

A large piece of Dark Empath's motives is that they are not being empathetic for the sake of being compassionate or altruistic. Their ability to relate and have cognitive empathy allows them to identify needs, insecurities, and desires in order to manipulate outcomes and emotions for their own benefit (Psych2Go). This means that underneath the desire to help, they can be callous and ruthless.

127

For some Dark Empaths, they might begin acts of kindness with good intentions, but over time those intentions can slip away. Underneath could be someone who cares, or someone who has unresolved trauma. Often folks with unresolved trauma have perceived drama with other people rather than self-reflecting and self-work, leading to a variety of complexes and refusal of accountability. The more malignant dark empaths can cognitively fit into empathic spaces, but not in a genuine way (Psych2Go). Their need to control the narrative or feel at the center makes them less of a healer and less of someone who would utilize their empathic abilities for the kind of good that is less about ego. An empath who is not dark would use their tools to promote the highest good, and not so much a self-serving outcome.

A dark empath can seem easygoing, until things don't go their way. Like some narcissists, they will charm you, put you on a pedestal, and make you feel like their top priority. Disagree with them, or point out a problem, and it is all of a sudden your fault. Quickly, the pedestal falls. There are Dark Empaths who will guilt trip and find a person's weakness in order to persuade them into doing what they want. They will also gaslight their way out of accountability, making the victim feel guilty for setting a boundary.

Various Archetypes

These descriptions are not meant to identify dark empaths as an exact science. They show us the type of toxic behaviors that exist in dark empaths, often additionally existing in some energy vampires and narcissists. Human behaviors have patterns and personality traits that group with other traits.

The Braggart

This type of Dark Empath likes to shove the Law of Attraction in your face. If bad things happen to you, it must mean that you have a worse relationship with the universe. They want to help you get better at your journey; they even have quite a few books to recommend to you.

This empath has been where you have been, or so they say. They want to compare you to old versions of themselves that they have shed. They have your number and know exactly what kind of person you are. Every resource they want to give you has been *life-changing*. They center themselves around your journey with an air of "Oh I'm so glad I am here so I can take care of you."

The Manipulator

These people are persuasive and know how to say just the right thing all too well. When they "ghost" you, they know they have to make you wonder where they went.

Manipulators are brilliant performers. They will act like something is completely torturing their soul, supplying crocodile tears in order to be given a break. They plan on getting what they want and do not play by the rules. Manipulators have the right amount of stubbornness and are dedicated if they have a high success rate.

The manipulator uses emotional intensity as punishment. They will react in such a way that is irresponsible or incoherent in a situation and uses a low emotional reaction in what happens to you. They might act cold or unconcerned. In contrast, they will have a highly accentuated reaction regarding themselves, which might present as panicked or worried.

To curb the outcome in their favor, the manipulator will use love bombing, ghosting, self-victimizing, intimidation, gaslighting, passive aggression, gossip, and intimidation.

They also use the exact language to make you feel like that bad guy or the lesser person. If you say _____,that makes you a psychopath." They may make you feel bad about your body. "Wow,

I didn't know you were still eating cake since, you know...." They try to compare you to others. "You're going to end up like your father."

Manipulators are not strangers. They have to know you are not going to run away. Already being in your head.

The Martyr

"The martyr sacrifices themselves entirely in vain. Or rather not in vain; for they make the selfish more selfish, the lazy more lazy, the narrow narrower." Florence Nightingale

When we say martyr here, we more or less mean someone with a martyr complex and not someone who is willing to die for their country. You have most likely met a martyr or someone who lives with a martyr. They may say things like "I have done everything for you," and will hold on to acts of service they committed, later to bring them up at a time that they can use to barter a favor later. The martyr will keep receipts and treat kindness like an accounting project.

It's odd because the martyr does not wait for consent to be helpful. They will help you excessively, whether you want it or not. Later they will say they have reached burnout and feel taken advantage of when they, in actuality, reached that point on their own, usually due to a lack of boundaries, the inability to say no, and the desire to want to complain about their plight later on.

This account is from Jamie, who had experienced Dark Empath behavior from her roommate, Rachel. Names have been changed to protect privacy.

Rachel and Jenna lived in a 6-person roommate situation with 4 adults and 2 children. Jenna was also an Empath. For the first year, Rachel was very understanding of Jenna's journey.

Rachel and another roommate, Gretchen, were not pleased with how Jenna and Michael did chores. They were not neglectful or lazy, they just prioritized differently. Rachel exploited the tension between Jenna and Gretchen to take her mind off her strained friendship with most of them.

Talk about a guilt trip... Rachel explained to Jamie the consequences of running out of firewood. The animals and children would freeze, and we could get called for neglect. Then Child Protection Services would be called. Mind you, that statement alone was a dramatic leap.

It was assumed that this was Jamie's designated chore, which was never communicated to Jamie. Either way, Rachel wanted to make sure Jamie got the consequences she felt Jamie deserved.

Another Martyr type, Mary, liked to tell her son's girlfriend how much of a good mother she was due to the number of sacrifices she had made for her son: Working multiple jobs, being a single parent, etc. She liked to self-compare her efforts to the girlfriend's mother, who had not been able to put her through college. Mary was sure to wonder out loud why the girlfriend's mother had not been more supportive.

While Mary was a self-proclaimed empath, she had forgotten one of the important rules of empathy, and that is understanding the broader scope of a person's life situation, and to be compassionate. Since the boyfriend was an only child, Mary only had to allocate funds to his care and education. The girlfriend had 3 other siblings, was the oldest, and her parents' divorce happened when she turned 15. As we know, divorces can be expensive, and being a single parent is an incredibly difficult path. Her mother had taken a hard financial hit due to the father's poor money management skills.

Martyrs in community service and volunteer groups sometimes have trouble understanding that other people have lives. The martyr may be the volunteer of the year. In their view, they are the most dedicated to the cause, because they *could* be with their family or with their dog, but instead, they choose to spend their precious time at the community center, where they want to make a difference. They will make a point of telling you so, and how little sleep they got that week.

The Entrepreneur

With the continuous wave of armchair psychology in blogs comes toxic positivity, which is a lucrative business for the entrepreneur archetype. When these articles, blogs, and novels in self-help were just one or two people, it was not a huge area of concern on a societal scale, but has since then become a cultural movement.

Entrepreneurs believe in one size fits all solutions to ailments, mental and physical.

They are either the leader of an MLM or an MLM's most recently converted prey. The Entrepreneur is a toxic positivity flavor that is smart, knows all the latest New Age buzzwords, and knows where your wallet meets your heart and sense of self-worth. This expensive gemstone store owner somehow knows you have "relationship conflict" in your life (a generic cold read).

Like the Braggart, the Entrepreneur loves to use the law of attraction to guilt people. The Law of Attraction was weaponized without considering institutionalized systems and poverty. Another unfortunate bias of the Entrepreneur is their tendency to think, "If I can do it, anyone can do it." Their empathy may be more geared toward being helpful in getting a person to heal and be successful, rather than acknowledging pain or obstacles.

The Entrepreneur, The Braggart, and the Medium archetypes often have a series of books and media that they collect to turn into a kind of religion centered around pseudoscience experts that further prey on recently divorced people looking for self-help novels.

Love bombing as a Strategy

The Love Bomber might wear you down with compliments, use flattery, or make you feel special. Once you feel content and joyful about the new relationship, they then pull the rug out from underneath you. The Love Bomber might end up needing something later. Often, in their own insecurity, the Love Bomber may rush relationships to gain a sense of stability, control, or comfort. They may not realize that they have attachment issues, or want to quickly move past the difficult parts of a relationship.

The Medium/The Mystic

The medium sometimes pairs with the Entrepreneur. The Medium can be an actual medium or someone who poses as having a channel to the spirit world in order to prey on vulnerable individuals that may be at rock bottom or who may be freshly grieving. Insecurity of the soul provokes mediums and entrepreneur archetypes to market their services to others the way one would sell makeup to people insecure about their skin.

Dark empaths can also exploit through grief, and many folks often wish they could contact their loved ones from beyond the grave. How do we know who is a real Medium? Let's be honest: we don't. Sometimes we have to go based on our personal experiences and trust. I typically go by level of theatrics and storytelling. Oppositely, I also go by generic statements and cold reading. What we wear and what makes our ears perk up are great tells for Mediums. You might be wearing a wedding ring, or have some genre of tattoo. Celebrity mediums are often skilled in the arts of body language and have powerful deduction skills that make a neat party trick. One should have a healthy bit of skepticism, just so that they are not lured into an expensive visit with their local psychic. Certain brands of faith healers feature speaking in tongues, false possessions, and so-called faith healings. Some of them use scams to bring dramatics into evoking emotional responses, all to turn a profit, not to contact your dearly departed.

My friend Kean once was a part of the after-hours portion of a metaphysical shop. By day, it was a spot for folks to grab their herbs, crystals, and whatnot. At night, a few people in the local pagan community would stay and perform rituals led by the shop owner, who was, supposedly, a self-proclaimed high priestess. He and his friend immediately saw the practices in her gaining loyalty from consumers and fan club members. When her leadership or "power" was questioned or challenged, she immediately went full Dark Empath mode.

A generic brand form of faith healing can be found in many arrays of money-draining metaphysical activities. This can take the form of Miracle cures from essential oils or various forms of "laying of the hands" healing.

The entrepreneur reminds me of the kind of church that promises that you are sealing some kind of contract with the universe or God through your dollars. This sadly still happens today.

"Pain Olympics" Champion

The pain Olympics champion can sometimes be a blended combination with the Martyr.

A Martyr is more ready to consent to suffering, but a pain Olympics person has often suffered a lot, and will vocalize this and make it clear that they will not go through it again. They ask that you respect them because they have suffered more. They ask for passes, excuses, freebies, and ways to get by rather than problem solve.

The champion will often chase after pain as well, and mistake a trauma response for having a "gut feeling about someone."

Many of these archetypes tend to forget the core of what it means to have empathy or to be an empath. Feeling what we feel or intimately knowing someone's pain does not license us to give help where unconsented. Being able to expedite our self-work or being able to heal and grow fast does not permit us to judge those who cannot do it at the same rate.

Questions for Reflection:

1. Do you think you have met at least one person in your life who may have been a dark empath? What were they like?
2. Do you worry that you may possess toxic, draining, or dark empath-like traits? What do you think you can do about it?
3. If the answer above is no, how do you operate that has convinced you that you are being the best person you can be?
4. Are there any people in your life that bring you the best joy and the worst kind of misery? Is that a healthy relationship?

3. Narcissists and Energy Vampires

"People inspire you or they drain you - pick them wisely."

— Hans F. Hansen

These kinds of people aren't always empaths or dark empaths, though narcissists share many of the dark triad traits with dark empaths, so there is some overlap. Energy vampires (sometimes known as psychic vampires), drain our prana, or life force energy. You may feel tired afterward. Sometimes mentally, sometimes physically. Around the energy vampire, you may feel that it is hard to be yourself.

For some people, energy vampirism appears as a personality trait or a chronic condition. It might also be that an energy vampire may be going through a rough patch, like a death in the family or a divorce. Some energy vampires know exactly what they are up to. Some often do not even know that they can sap the energy from others in a room. People that are naturally negative to the extreme might not realize they are killing the vibe in the room.

Some energy vampires are full of drama. They feel very strongly that the drama is real and seismic. Every conflict they experience is a crisis. They may be doing this for attention, or to remove the need to handle their real problems. A crisis is so much more interesting than a mundane task or a financial issue. There are some that are quite aware of how much they hyperbolize the drama. They become addicted to the attention, sympathy, and compassion of others. My friend Thalia used to work for a lady who owned a new age spa with massage, Reiki, and acupuncture. The owner was always late and tended to always have her cancellations and tardiness attached to a crisis or an excuse. This often came with an air of "I need to make forgiving me your problem, rather than changing behavior my problem." If Thalia or a coworker became angry for her lateness due

136

to (supposedly) an unexpected event, they would appear inflexible or callous, which is an unfair bind to be in.

As you have probably recognized, not all energy vampires are malicious people with the intent to harm. Many just get caught up in their own lives and forget to be considerate and share space. We probably meet our first energy vampire on the playground. Someone who would not share, or someone who tattled on every single kid to gain favor with the teacher. Depending on nature, nurture, and the number of boundaries, obstacles, and challenges a person has faced, people act in this manner for a reason. Some of them were not given the opportunity to learn emotional intelligence, build resilience, or learn how to communicate and build authentic connections.

The "Yes, but" kind of person has an additional comment for everything, whether it's informative, fueled by worry, or a need to control the situation. They may feel the need to be Devil's advocate. They want things "to be fair" even when the devil does not need any help or a debate is not a balanced argument.

Another "yes, but..." type can never just say yes to something due to paranoia, fear, mistrust, or anxiety. Complications feel important because there is value in solving a problem, and pessimism feels like being prepared. It happens a lot in creative spaces; it's not enough to accept an idea, you have to criticize it in the same breath.

Out there in the world, and probably your life, there are additionally needy friends, chatty Cathy's, or chronic talkers. These folks might resemble energy vampires, but usually a few quick conversations and established boundaries, and you can have your ears back.

The energy vampire will bring you problems and complaints but no solutions. They may gossip about good news, bad news, juicy news, or anything that changes the energy in a room. Energy vampires like to take up space. They like to take a conversation and

137

make it about a topic specific to their interests. They will not have a sense of mindfulness of the time or what percentage of the conversation they are taking up. They want to be heard, regardless of their position. Some are also the "to be fair type" in a debate. A devil's advocate will make up a position to have it for the sake of debate and contrarianism. They see conversation as a game. They want to win no matter what the sides are. In their view, unsupported opinions deserve as much airtime and weight as fact or more provable and examined opinions.

Energy vampires mistrust, and want a padlock on the faculty lounge refrigerator in fear of their lunch getting stolen. Oppositely, some energy vampires are freeloaders and absolutely will take food in a public or private space if no boundaries are presented.

While energy vampires prefer to be seen and heard, it is definitely on their terms. They are not open books. They will be late to parties and make it everyone else's problem for not bringing the game or a specific item they promised to bring.

There was a roommate who used to live with my friend Shawn. The roommate would go into the apartment with a big gray cloud. This guy's mood told you if Raymond ain't happy, ain't nobody happy. They have a problem with other people having happiness or a good day because they are having a miserable one. Shawn would have to hole himself up in his bedroom, just to get some peace and not accidentally take on too much of Raymond's stale energy. Raymond would sulk around the apartment, order a whole lot of take-out, and rarely helped clean the toilet or take out the recycling.

In a more comical example, Colin Robinson is a type of energy vampire in "What We Do in the Shadows." Though more of a hyperbolic and archetypal example, Colin is the perfect example of an energy vampire. Colin directly and aggressively takes space, attention, and resources. Resources do not have to be money. He takes up his friends' emotional resources and attention span. He gets in the way of television screens. He is the "Well, actually..." type and has some kind of knowledge or advice to share, even if it is not asked for.

In the chapter, "Protecting Yourself and Setting Boundaries", you are presented with a more in-depth look at what it means to protect yourself in both a general and specific sense. For our purposes here, here are some specific ways to deal with an energy vampire.

Since some energy vampires have no idea that they are draining you, it may be a good idea to simply step away or make an excuse to leave. Sometimes they just get caught in a negative feedback loop and need to be interrupted in order to move on to the next task or activity.

Other energy vampires that try to push your buttons should not be "fed" so to speak, as in, do not react. If they can not get a reaction out of you, they cannot witness something bothering you. If they are cornering you with negativity or complaining, offering solutions can be helpful. The point here is not to solve the problem for them. The purpose is to get them out of the feedback loop of complaining, and either move on or realize you are not going to engage in the way they want you to.

Do not have a concern with being right with energy vampires. They will take that inch of doubt or disagreement and take it a mile. They want to come out at the end and feel victorious, and their usual method is to wear you down or use logical fallacies. It also helps to not get defensive, for this is another sign that they are pushing your buttons.

What if you are an energy vampire?

If you are stressed, or not taking proper care of yourself, there is a chance you will lean into some energy vampire tendencies. You may complain a lot to your friends. You might be checking your face in the mirror a lot and asking friends for validation and compliments about your physical appearance. If you become the town or workplace gossip, people may start to avoid you or not make eye contact with you. You may find people not confiding in you as much. You may not be giving people any place to celebrate or give news without being critical or pessimistic.

Your friend says, "We're engaged!"

You say, "Great! I hope it lasts!"

What a way to kill the mood and throw a backhanded compliment!

What do you do when you become an energy vampire? Fear not, for you are not cursed into energy-sucking vampirism for all eternity. Once you become more self-aware, you will be able to catch yourself reaching burnout, emotional exhaustion, or anything that might lead to consuming the good vibes in the room.

To avoid energy vampire tendencies, make sure you both practice self-care and are aware of your social habits with others. Make sure in conversations that you listen with patience, without interrupting, and without critique. Stick to the facts and try not to go into theatrics. Do not complain too much about one thing for an extended period. Furthermore, try to find spots of gratitude or spots to breathe in your day.

Narcissists

Narcissists love for the attention to be on them. They do not care about sharing or contributing. We often think of narcissists in relation to the Greek legend of Narcissus, who loved looking at his reflection. He ignored the cries of Echo, which angered Nemesis, the god of revenge. He was cursed to fall in love with the next person he saw, which was his face in the water.

Real narcissists are not only self-absorbed by their looks alone. The personality traits of a narcissist are defined by grandiosity, self-centeredness, lack of self-reflection, and not engaging in symbiotic behavior. They believe they deserve only the best. They will ask for favors and sharing, but will not share or contribute. If they see an easy way out, they shall take it. Here, Narcissism is part of the Dark Triad for a reason. It is a very dangerous and destructive personality and can lead to abusive, unfulfilling, or one-sided relationships. Narcissists are defined by hypersensitivity, ego-centricity, grandiosity, manipulation, lack of empathy, seeking admiration and validation seeking, rage, entitlement, exploitation, and superficiality.

Narcissists tend to community surf. They arrive and act like a big shot. When their plan to charm everyone and get away with emotionally swindling people finally starts to backfire and become unbalanced, they then leave to create division or drama in another community. Narcissists are hypersensitive and do not take criticism well, and are prone to mood swings. They put others down and take advantage of people.

My theater friends tell me of the number of narcissists that do this from community theater to community theater. They throw fits when they do not get the part they want. They go to any audition presenting themselves in the manner of "do you even know who I am?"

Some were predatory, preying on the most vulnerable actors and actresses, particularly younger women that were barely of age. They demonstrate other behaviors as well. They will show up, take the spotlight, gain power, Any demand for accountability means they just bounce to another place to dismantle.

Narcissists know that there is a need to target people who do not know them not well enough to set a boundary or give feedback, it gives a specific view of who they are, less vulnerability, and more control. It is acceptable for them to demand your attention, but not for you to demand theirs.

Narcissists tend to target naive or vulnerable people. In naive people, there is so much they do not yet know about how the world operates. Their innocence and lack of street smarts, cultural smarts, or tendency to see the best in people means that they are more likely to be taken advantage of by a narcissist. To be clear, there is nothing wrong with seeing the best in people, but it is not wise to trust everyone unconditionally.

Narcissism can be classified as a childhood and developmental thing to some degree. While it does not excuse the behavior, it helps to know where the choices made by a narcissist come from. When diagnosed, there is a known block in development in which the adult continues to feel a sense of grandiosity and self-importance that has little room for others. They may have witnessed poorly demonstrated behaviors. Their parents may have given them excessive praise. Whatever the cause, many narcissists have incredibly high self-esteem, but only due to an inflated ego and a skewed perception of their successes, which appear grand to them (Britannica). This high self-esteem can flip-flop from day to day, with insecurities flooding in if their ego has not been satiated or inflated for some time.

Narcissism might be preventable for some parents. One of the root causes might be too much praise or putting the child on a pedestal. Another cause of narcissism might be a lack of warmth in parenting, with the narcissist traits developing due to a void that was formed in childhood from lack of praise, positive interactions, or mutual joy between them and their parents (Brummelman).

Either way, budding narcissists seem to have a form of entitlement, whether they feel like they never got enough attention, or if they have been consistently been informed that they are the best at what they do.

Symbiosis is not in the best interests of the narcissists, for they expect you to spend more energy than them. They operate on such a low-frequency energy, you can feel your energy being sapped, especially when you notice they are not doing their share in the relationship.

A narcissist prefers to bring others down, rather than raise them up, unless they choose to engage in a need or want on their personal list. Making someone feel special one day and useless the next is their forte. They will instill fear in you so that you think that there will be only one person who wants to put up with you and your flaws. They control the narrative and know what they are doing, wanting to persuade you or influence your next move, get your fear and anxiety up. When your fear is heightened, it makes it easier to manipulate you.

Many feel a need to control others, so they manipulate by any means necessary, including being domineering or destructive. They will want to control the narrative and paths to knowledge so that you have to rely on them for wisdom and clarity. They will infantilize you or make you question your own intelligence, memory, and sanity. They might make many rules, or generate a kind of bureaucracy, semantics, rules lawyering, and pedantry when communicating. Creating hoops to jump through gives them a thrill.

So why do we put up with all of this? Often when we first encounter a narcissist, they hit us with charm, charisma, and confidence. This is a seductive cloud that causes us to look through rose-colored glasses.

The act of gaslighting also contributes to why some people stay around narcissists longer than intended. Gaslighting questions your intelligence, makes you feel crazy, or can lead you to become dependent on an abuser. What if you're nothing without them? What if you deserve the way they are treating you? Does this sound healthy or right?

The aesthetic narcissist finds their way into spaces of fashion, make-up, fitness gyms, arts, and even at the family barbeque. Their obsession with fitness or physical appearance will often be fueled by feeling prettier and healthier than others.

A Note on Youth

As adults, we may be sensitive to behaviors that appear to be that of narcissists and energy vampires. When this appears in a child or teenager, we may react in a way as though we are speaking to an adult who knows better. It is important to be mindful that their brains are not fully developed, and it is up to us to guide, mentor, and lead by example. We may put up a boundary that demonstrates emotional regulation, or we might have to have a conversation with our kids as to why it is important to have boundaries.

You might explain to them about having a friend over to your house. Say the friend starts just going through your fridge, eating everything without asking. There are a few ways to react to the situation. You could let them continue eating. You could leave the room and pretend you did not notice. You could shove them out. You could set a boundary, by saying, "Hey, I'd like you to stop. There's only a certain amount I have for the week, or that my family needs. Next time you're hungry please ask first."

When a child negatively reacts to something, we might get triggered by it from our past traumas or expectations. Rather than calling them ungrateful, lazy, or names that are never helpful, you might desire a conversation with them about what your boundary setting looks like. You can ask that you both calm down before the problem-solving is resumed. Tune into your feelings.

Redfield's Archetypes

From James Redfield's *The Celestine Prophecy,* there are some specific energy vampires to become aware of:

There is the Intimidator, who gains energy by intimidating others. They often make others feel inferior and can be verbally or physically aggressive (Redfield). You may often see an Intimidator at the grocery store or a retail store. If they are having a bad day, they are likely to take out their frustration on a cashier, or the next person that mildly inconveniences them. Intimidators like to be in control and feel unopposed. They are unlikely to listen to reasoning, logic, and rationality when someone takes the time to explain what is happening.

The next energy stealer is known as the Interrogator, who is critical and may ask questions that they consider to come from a place of care, but often carry an air of putting the focus on their ego. These folks often take pride in debating or playing devil's advocate. They also may ask you passive or directly aggressive questions like, "Oh, you spent money on *that*?", "Why aren't you engaging with me?!" (often mentioned in a debate), or "That shirt is rather tight around you. Do you know of any fitness gyms around here?" They often carry the kind of narcissistic advice that tells you, "My [moral/fitness/financial/etc.] choices are better than yours." "You have to rely on my judgment." "You can't make good decisions without me."(Eddy) Moral superiority is an issue that empaths should also look out for, for they can easily fall into such feelings when making mindful, active, and healthy life choices.

You would think this next energy vampire would not be someone who drains you: The Aloof. An Aloof has usually come from an abusive parent or partner. They act cagey and are very hard to read. When working cooperatively, they do not seem keen on being the person who leads or makes key decisions. They would rather not tell people what they honestly think, and may give vague responses like "I guess" or "Maybe" or "I don't know". (Croft) We tend to feel the most for The Aloof. We may want desperately for them to gain confidence, or try to coach them in standing up for themselves or being heard. In a workplace or romantic partner scenario, you will carry the mental load of decision-making or propelling choices forward.

The last and fourth vampire type is The Poor Me. Poor Mes are your whiners, and folks with victim complexes. These people take the victim position, saying their life is unfair and no one wants to support them, even if they are well supported. Poor Me energy vampires will often make the other person feel guilty. They will use their predicaments and drama to manipulate others into helping them.

If we can recognize we are being drained and sharing our energy, we can more readily put up energetic walls that protect us from folks that may be willfully or unintentionally stealing our energy (Croft).

I once met a Reiki master who explained that the higher your frequency, the more likely you are to attract toxicity and energy that does not belong in your various auric and energetic fields. The light of an empath is like a bulb that attracts moths and flies. The more you can prepare and fortify yourself like a well-guarded castle, the more you can propel the flies, or more appropriately, mosquitos.

Questions for Reflection:

1. What do your body, mind, and spirit feel like after an energy vampire encounter?
2. Do you think there have been times where you might have been an energy vampire, or at the very least, sucked a little bit of the energy out of the room?
3. What are some healthy boundaries you can set up around energy vampires and narcissists?

4. Not All Archetypes Are Black & White: The Gray Area

We could also refer to the "gray area" as the at-risk zone for empaths. Highly sensitive folks and empaths in this category are usually not too far gone...yet, but they are on the dangerous road sometimes towards becoming a dark empath or energy vampire.

The effects of acting on empathy might come from a sense of validation or feeling needed.

The Savior

I have seen many empaths in the educator communities fall into savior complexes. Many of these individuals tend to work in American public schools at either the elementary level or the secondary level. They want to "save" every kind of student. The kids in poverty, who are disabled, who have a hard home situation, etc. Many teachers dream of becoming the role-model teacher from Freedom Writers, or Dead Poets Society, or Stand and Deliver. Unfortunately, life is not a Lifetime original film, and administration is less flexible with educators that use unorthodox methods to get their class to improve and be responsive.

Savior types want to make everything go well. They feel like they can't leave or that they are responsible for the outcome. Many teachers have a hard time calling in sick because they feel needed by their school or their kids.

The Fixer/The Burnout

The fixer wants their friends, parents, and coworkers to be happy. You find them always giving/volunteering their time to people they are close to. This is often a symptom of a poor self-image. If one can not be of service, or is not needed, they feel worthless.

A fixer also cannot pour from an empty cup. Being a fixer may lead to a case of martyrdom or, you guessed it, burnout, so self-care is very important.

The *Really* Good Listener

You may have been told many times, even by strangers, that you are a good listener. It might even feel easy. You walk away, surprisingly unweighted by what they just told you. If anything, you feel amazing. You feel elevated and energized. You were there for someone. You felt needed. And you got to learn something new.

There is a fundamental part of our psyche that has a need or several needs. We feel like we must meet that need at any cost. For some folks, it's travel, or physical fitness, or sexual gratification. It can really be anything. Some of these needs are easy to fulfill. Some are not. It depends on socioeconomic status, realistic probability, gender, cultural norms, and general accessibility. Sometimes a need to be fulfilled can be impossible or to our detriment, especially if it is something like wealth, needing to travel to an expensive island every year, or needing today a specific kind of partner with specific physical traits.

Unfortunately, listening to people's problems is a need that can be met infinitely, and folks that become addicted to being a listening ear will keep looking for it to meet that need.

You may reach a point where you realize you were not even listening, you were just being *fed.*

The Bleeding Heart

A bleeding heart gives and gives often. A bleeding heart would be not comfortable in a community that was not hurting. Their gut instinct to feel hurt on behalf of humanity would not be triggered all the time in a calm, low crisis space. They may be at risk of moving toward the status of holier than thou types, who lose their purpose in peace and would rather appear righteous and dedicated as part of their vanity.

The bleeding heart walks a line of guilt, compassion, love, sameness, otherness, and discomfort. The difference between an altruistic bleeding heart and an inauthentic one is how they respond to their empathy and discomfort tied to it. An altruistic, authentic bleeding heart does not want humanity to suffer, and it is as simple as what. They want to help for the sake of helping. An inauthentic bleeding heart is performative and over-centers themselves and their ego. You may see this with people who do residencies, missionary work, and voluntourism. Some of them take selfies with "poor" African children or take proud selfies of themselves with wreckage from a hurricane behind them. Following the principles of Atticus Finch (if you get the reference from *To Kill a Mockingbird*), it is better to just do the good work quietly and maybe unnoticed, rather than to parade around your self-imposed courageousness for clout and the number of likes and thumbs-ups that you earn at the expense of someone else's suffering.

In contrast, the authentic bleeding heart person tends to be involved in humanitarian projects and is very vocal about their ties to social justice. Because they are not at the holier than thou stage, they mean well in their commitments. They truly want the world to be a better place. The news absolutely destroys their day. Multiple instances of human suffering, and the bleeding heart may feel inclined to take the rest of the day off of work. The world's distress is their distress. They allow their thoughts to be filled with crying children, starving populations, and warring countries.

It is not helpful to dwell on the amount of impact one cannot make on their own and to instead focus energy on the little everyday actions and miracles that we can perform in our community. To take the world's problems and put them on our shoulders leads to those awful feelings of hopelessness.

149

Questions for Reflection:

Do any of the gray area archetypes resonate with you? Do you think this may be a good yellow light for you to slow down?

What is an alternative to being a constant fixer or bleeding heart?

What do all of these archetypes have in common?

5. Avoiding Martyrdom

"A thing is not necessarily true because a man dies for it."

— *Oscar Wilde*

Martyrdom is very often self-imposed, so it is avoidable. Those who work in health care, therapy, human services, and social services can experience martyr-like issues and feelings. They may not take care of themselves in the same way they would their patients or clients. They may feel an obligation to continue to put their needs last.

A first step is to be the person that does not remind others that they owe you one. When we use phrases like "after all I did for you," it can lock another person into a place of guilt that is manipulative and unfair. People who want to have every favor be transactional turn out to be emotional loan sharks that expect special treatment or hero treatment.

Many people approaching a martyr complex hope to feel appreciated or noticed. Is there a way perhaps that we can use our own gratitude in our actions, rather than fishing for compliments or recognition. We can also understand that people show gratitude in different ways. A lot of people hope for a "thank you," but sometimes gratitude might not be shown that day. Maybe the enjoyment of an activity or an invitation somewhere can be a sign of gratitude. Say you clean someone's house, and they invite you to dinner again. Reciprocity is another example, especially when the behavior at the right time seems massive or worthless, so you do not see it. Or asking how you are doing, and checking in. Understand also that people aren't always going to show gratitude. It is not that they do not feel it, or even if they are preoccupied by other things, it does not mean you are ruined as a helpful human being. Sometimes there is just satisfaction in knowing you made someone's day.

Another way one can avoid martyrdom is to stop attempting the mind-reading of needs. They assume their friends are struggling with something via perception, which is often skewed. Many martyr types are also fixers, which means they love to attract conflict that they feel obligated to fix. Those who take on a hostess hub of conflict like to be the advice giver, centering themselves in the conflict by playing the mediator, but more often the instigator. They may see problems that are not even there. My friend's mother-in-law put herself in the center of her son's relationship, planting ideas in his head that were likely untrue about the relationship.

Questions for Reflection:

1. How can we acknowledge our own work without seeking validation or witnessing from others?
2. How can you express your needs so that you do not become a martyr?
3. If you are meeting someone's needs and yours are not reciprocated, why do you feel the need to stay in the pattern? Is there a way you can communicate inside the relationship, or make a change?

6. Avoiding The "Holier than Thou" Trap

"Happy people don't go through life collecting and seeking recognition. They go through life giving it away."

— Dodinsky

The desire to help others can be its own brand of addiction without proper boundaries and awareness of one's own limitations. Some folks hurt others or genuinely want to help; this is not a negative thing, but it is important to have it continue to come from a place of compassion and not a place of just wanting to "look good."

Having the bandwidth to take care of others is a lovely blessing, but not if it is used in a manner in which no one asked. Being the pinnacle of humanitarianism does not win you a gold star. Moral superiority and self-righteousness are not meant to guide one when making a change or doing good for the community. People tend to follow by example, not by performance.

Holier than thou types participate in transactional accounting, keeping score on all favors and actions done for the benefit of specific people. Out of nowhere, if asked a favor, they suddenly know every favor done for you over the last five years. If they are confronted with boundaries or complaints, you will get hit with the "After all I've done for you,." speech. They keep "receipts for years.

How do we prevent ourselves from keeping Random Acts Of Kindness receipts? We can hope that those we assist, pay it forward, and understand the benefit of our kindness may not directly come back to us. We can choose to take personal satisfaction in knowing how it happened, like a playful secret. You may also ask yourself why is it so important that someone acknowledges you?

It is hard to guilt people into buying more ethically. It is a bit of a trap when you consider how poverty works. To choose between buying ethically grown coffee and an ethically made in the US t-shirt...both are twenty dollars, but you could get both for a generic brand price at $6.99 and $10 at the thrift store. Not everyone has access to funds, academic knowledge, resources, Community, and so they may not have the Bandwidth to follow it to a tee.

A holier than thou type of person gives their time or does an act of kindness, or favor, and then selects what hurts and offends them after they have given. Being a volunteer of the year or a good community member entitles them to be treated well.

Another kind of holier-than-thou person taps heavily into acting as the positivity police. A phrase that is being used more and more in the zeitgeist is toxic positivity. Many folks that get into self-help books or new age spiritual movement philosophies sometimes end up on the wrong end of it. Yes, you likely found this very book on a self-improvement shelf, but the last thing I want is for you to act more enlightened and improved than everyone else. Everyone is on their own journey at their own pace. We do not need to preach what we learned from a book when it is a better use of our time to continue to use the knowledge on ourselves to become the best version of ourselves.

Often, a person riding on toxic positivity will be very into the Law of Attraction, often blaming another person for the negative things that happen in their life on their own negativity or perspective. In reality, this same person will ignore the actual causes and effects of their lives, including their own behavior or yours. Being positive becomes more important than growth, change, and accountability, as negativity, or anything that isn't upbeat or optimistic, is the sole enemy. There is no accounting for luck (good or bad), or being in the wrong place at the wrong time. Being positive does not necessarily mean a person is doing well either. You can be positive and still be late for work, flake on assignments, or not have any follow-through as a person. Depression is considered a low-vibrational emotion, which sounds very stigmatic of a mental illness. It is better to feel our emotions and process them. Sadness is not a low-vibrational feeling; it is simply a natural response to death, disappointment, a relationship change, or moving.

Going back to the law of attraction and attracting abundance: socioeconomic status takes a large role in how people get access to the things that make it easy to live their life. Grants, inheritance, lucky situations, and settlements are things only a rare few people get. Then, there are systems in place that do not make it such a cookie-cutter recipe for similar paths to success. Not everyone has those opportunities. Rather than assuming that folks have the means to manifest, or be more confident, or pull themselves up by the bootstraps, it is important to keep Maslow's hierarchy of needs in mind: if a person's physiological and/or safety needs are not met, we can not possibly expect them to have good self esteem or to self-actualize.

It takes a certain kind of person to have the energy, patience, skillset, and time to work with children, homeless people, terminally ill people, traumatized people, victims of natural disasters, folks in hospice, refugees, or any other kind of vulnerable person. These are often a manner of demeanor and cability, not moral constitution. Some people have the stomach or proper mental guard to see humanity in its most distressed forms.

There is additionally the kind of holier-than-thou person that is socially aware, politically aware, academically aware and culturally aware. They think they know the best circumstances and ideal living situations for everyone, and what it would take for all of humanity to get on board and make change. While this is a noble cause, some people in this crowd will belittle and insult others who do not fully understand cause and effect concepts. This could be due to a lack of exposure or education. Anyone who is "ignorant" of "common sense" is meant to wear the social dunce cap due to a lack of not widely known knowledge. Which brings another thought - is what is common sense for us, based on our lived experience, common sense for someone else? Is there a way we can educate without insulting another's intelligence? Is there a way we can inform without shaming someone for forgivable amounts of inexperience? (Willful ignorance is an exception, of course.)

Expecting ourselves to do better is a wonderful thing, but putting the same expectation on others can be unfair when we do not know much about their life or limitations.

Questions for Reflection:

Is there a way to feel good about what you are doing without guilting others?

Can you be grateful for your space, resources, and privilege to help people without condemning your peers?

If you know someone who acts 'holier than thou', how might you inform them that not everyone has the same life, time, or resources? If you are not in a space where you can inform, how can you create an energetic distance to protect yourself?

7. The Use and Abuse of Empathy in the Business World

"The most truly generous persons are those who give silently without hope of praise or reward."

– Carol Ryrie Brink

Empathy has a lot of uses in the business world. Current professional development techniques include trying to practice active listening, compassion, and patience. They suggest that professionals adjust to work styles and accommodate worker needs.

As important as it is to care about your staff's wants and needs, it is also important to consider your consumers' wants and needs. What is most ergonomic about the product? What is affordable? What is accessible?

Empathetic bosses listen without judgment and do not gossip. They ask for explanations and clarification rather than getting defensive or pulling a power move. Employers who give room for addressing concerns are going to boost staff morale. If their partner is in the hospital, or their child's care is unavailable, be understanding if they need to work from home or find a way to let the child come to work.

Empathy in business is also heavily abused. We witness the product world with its diet products, quick solutions, and general habit of getting away with making us feel terrible about our bodies, choices, and lifestyles. Questionable charities use sad footage and music to get us to donate to their cause which often receives a small fraction of the donations. There are thankfully websites these days that can tell you how much is spent in non-profit budgets like the CEO's paycheck, marketing, the cause, research, etc.

The empathy deficit in business and jobs is getting recognized. An executive's ego, opinion, expertise, and attachment to being right seem to be more valued than empathizing with others who may have diverging mindsets. Hard-charging entrepreneurs find it hard to let go of their status or set aside the lessons learned as they came up through the ranks. Executives and managers lose touch with the experiences, perceptions, and perspectives of customers, employees, and stakeholders. We see this in schools when laws are passed by people who have so much administrative distance from the buildings, the students, the staff, and the curriculum. Data like that from test scores are used for making decisions about children who have holistic and complex education needs, and that same data is used to put pressure on teachers to do well, lest their job be put in jeopardy.

The algorithm of how the internet uses your information and interests is highly predatory. Empathy is not just about making you feel sad. If you see someone who looks like you or shares your aesthetic looking happy, enjoying life with the brightly colored and well-lit product, something in your brain is going to tell you that you *have* to have that dress. If you see a person experiencing depression over a problem in a grayscale commercial, switching to a sunny colorful day once the problem is solved by the pill, the sad scene might pull at your core in some way if you also experience or have experienced the same ailment.

How fascinating is it that we are asked to give our dollars and attention to celebrities, politicians, and costumed face characters, but not given enough time to visit those we would rather care for? When we are not working, we are consuming, and when we are not consuming, we are resting, and it becomes this cycle that becomes very difficult to get out of. Capitalism is about the bottom line, with each measure being based on how we capture someone's attention, wallet, votes, or labor, especially if the labor is cheap.

There are some feel-good stories about empathetic bosses and CEOs finally doing something empathetic or at the very least beneficial for their staff. One boss told their employees it was okay if they arrived late or missed a day, as long as the work got done. People have children, emergencies, elderly parents, and medical appointments. One should not have to go into debt or get punished if they put family and life first.

Another CEO took a hit from their salary (which was already in the hundreds of millions) so that their employees could earn a livable wage. They later found out that this move increased morale, lessened turnover, and even boosted productivity.

The Shady Entrepreneurs and Suck Up Coworkers.

Some Dark Empaths use their niceness to please coworkers and superiors of higher status. Your coworker may have not filed their paperwork a day correctly their entire life, but they suck up so well to the boss, they are now golf buddies. They may have charmed the secretary into accepting their reports late. Maybe they have convinced their shift supervisor to be easygoing on tasks, because of some theatrical story about a recent injury or something oh so sad on their mind.

Shady entrepreneurs are those who use Empathy to gain approval, buy, and fulfill orders. Their tendency to say no means they may reach burnout, and not deliver expectations in a timely manner. They may have a sincere need for attention (Psych2Go) You see entrepreneurs on stages at conventions and expos, often surrounded by budding entrepreneurs. They have no problem getting work or offers. They give the act of fairness, of wanting to cut you a good deal.

At the current writing of this book, more companies have been realizing that Empathy is profitable, both in the genuine sense and, more dangerously, in the exploitative sense.

Reiki Master or Con Artists? Gurus or Appropriators?

Many creatives, sensitives, and empaths need community. This is true of most humans, but empaths may actively seek it out from the need to feel seen or understood. They are presented with unique mental toolboxes, and finding like-minded individuals can be a bit of a trap when predatory people operate in the businesses that empaths are drawn to.

Eastern practices have become very attractive to those who wish to access healing and broaden their horizons. While it can be beneficial for holistic and integrative healing, these practices are often paired with space presented and curated by energy vampires and Dark Empaths. Remember that archetype that is an Entrepreneur? The Entrepreneur is not necessarily a person of ethics. They are often very charming, motivating, and manipulative. The Entrepreneur will fleece the herd of fans or followers, conning their income consistently from folks that look to them as a mentor or leader type. Some Entrepreneurs are not necessarily in it for the money. They may prefer raking in glory, status, attention, or just a general following. This does not necessarily make their practices ethical or unethical.

In Yoga studios, for example, the general intention is to emulate the aesthetic of traditional Asian cultures. These are used to create an atmosphere that emulates a safe and healing space. Whether this intention is genuine or not, it can sometimes lead to the same kinds of judgemental communities found in Western faith-based circles, such as a Catholic book club or a Homeowners Association. This is logistically incompatible with the Asian cultures that we take for aesthetics, but do not adopt meaningful philosophy or lesson learning.

There are those who would also utilize our empathy for profit, particularly in the self-help and multi-level marketing industry. One might hear buzz words like "attracting abundance" paired with a kind of shame if one is not able to do this on their own. They may be encouraged to buy more products and subscribe to more groups.

Exploiting New Age Empath

Setting reasonable boundaries with any dark empath or energy vampire can mean backlash. You may be accused of being too negative and maybe excommunicated from the group you once felt safe in.   This is usually a "shun the non-believer" kind of strategy.

Yoga and meditation Studios will often have affordable classes for daily exercise but will lure customers into expensive getaways, courses, and so on.

Have you ever found out when the shop owner says, the crystals speak to you and then you realize you are holding on to the most expensive one? Disregarding the fact that many gems are not ethically sourced, but as lovely as stones and crystals are, I do not think they actually "speak" to you when you buy them. It's the equivalent of saying a trendy new t-shirt is calling your name. Shopkeepers know this, for they want you to feel a connection to the thing they want you to buy. You have to feel it in your soul so much, you are overcome with emotion when you purchase that lapis lazuli pyramid. Even if you are someone with an affinity for gemstones, the best metaphysical experts will tell you that you only need a mere fragment of a stone, not one large enough to be a coffee table.

Politics and Non for Profits

In order to gain popularity, votes, or funds, some parties will weaponize empathy to sway the public. While they are tapping into your emotions, guilt is often the product. If politicians and advertising are essentially the same in the free market (your attention, your money, your votes), then empathy in those spaces is built on creating a problem.

You see a heartbreaking commercial about the planet or the starving children. You feel bad about it. Then, the next talking point in the commercial is to sell you a solution in order to feel better about it.

Our hardwired empathy means making the problem by 'informing you' or making you worry about a new thing or an old one, and that moment of feeling bad is easy to exploit. we may be empathic by instinct, and our need to 'feel better' is also an instinct. vote, spend, etc.

Is it also fair to ask the same populations who live paycheck to paycheck as the folks who have income beyond occasional disposable income?

The people who are going to feel it the hardest are the people who can empathize, because they have been in a similar position, or know someone close to them who has suffered like the person/people on the screen.

Some philosophers suggest if we allow free will to be a critical component in all of this, you cannot manipulate someone into doing something kind. They must actively choose to take action, or not, in which case the class of the person doesn't quite matter. They will give because they want to or feel bad. It's just a moral question of what will raise the most money or "do the most good." The philosophers further suggest if you know a person is likely to donate because of their empathy, you cannot take advantage of them if you admit that obeying their empathy or acting on it is their own choice by their consent. You are not successful in finding the most capable or affluent humans, you are just playing the cards well to see what sticks or generates dollars.

What if, on the other hand, empathy is treated more as a controlling force that can create such an intense feeling that a person can't help themselves, then it is coercion to some degree, right? We must be careful not to center free will as the driving force above all other things because then it blames people who take their own actions seemingly without persuasion or coercion, even if they were manipulated subliminally or worn down with repetition of the same dumb ad.

I suspect some places don't mean to exploit us in this manner, but they must in the inherent process of their work and effort. "We need money to save this village. Let's tell people about the village and they will want to help' and the 'want to help' is code for, being guilted or persuaded into giving money. Who knows if this is done ethically because we are not in the room when this happens.

Questions for Reflection:

1. Have you ever been taken advantage of due to your capacity to care about humanity?
2. How can folks build community and help others without using guilt?
3. Have you ever found a hobby or group that you thought had the same ethics and values as you, and it turned out they were more gimmicky, gatekeeping, and guilt-tripping than you originally thought?

8. Altruism and Compassion

"The thing is, I don't do these things for recognition, being a good teammate, being a positive member of the community. I do them because those things make me whole and complete."

–Dwyane Wade

No one can be nice or kind without having a hidden motivation, right? Not necessarily. Speak with pessimists, and they view that other humans are fueled by greed, lust, and a desire for power. Speak with certain kinds of mentors, monks, and philosophers, and that view may be challenged often.

Some empaths have a sincere desire to prevent and circumvent as little suffering in the world as possible.

Altruism involves non-transactional generosity and energy. A good deed done is not mentioned publicly. One simply does the thing they hope might do good, and then goes about their day. Altruistic folks know that kindness is meant to be a habit, both in public and behind closed doors. It is not meant to be used as a tool for building a reputation. If a person feels true empathy, it is the kind that is an authentic, respectful connection to another person's situation. Altruism is then just the golden rule- treat them as you want to be treated, because in a sense, they are you and you are them, or at least your perception of life has allowed you to see it that way.

It is also possible perhaps altruism, true altruism, is fully singular- a thing a community does to itself, rather than an arrangement of smaller one-on-one moments. an extension of multiple people caring for themselves as a group, rather than 'i am altruistic', which even as a statement is a selfish act in most cases, as you would not be inclined to point it out, as it goes against the very nature of altruism.

164

Altruistic folks believe in good neighbor practices and not the kind of model, "concerned" citizen that energy vampires take on. There is an offering to trim your neighbor's hedges, and then there is the kind of person who criticizes your pets, the toys on your lawn, the people you have over, and the length of your grass. Either they love being smug about the quality of their own home, or they have nothing better to do.

Engage in conversation in a non consensual manner, putting you in a bind because you do not want to be rude to the person who lives next door.

An altruistic neighborhood has a community garden, but not the kind with a padlock or a barbed-wire fence. It gives a certain kind of mistrust.

Altruism encourages prosocial behavior, which is a social action or behavior that benefits other people or society as a whole. This can appear as helping, sharing, collaborating, and volunteering. We find this in shared spaces, community gardens, artist collectives, and libraries. We can also find this in non-profits that do not have hidden agendas or enrich their own staff at the cost of the cause. Encouraging prosocial behavior can be difficult in places where altruism and emotional intelligence are lacking. In a me-first world or a self-serving culture, the health, prosperity, or overall happiness of the group does not matter.

There are a few religions, philosophies, schools of thought, etc. that examine human suffering and have resolved to reduce that suffering or provide change. This includes Buddhism, Negative Utilitarianism, and Negative Consequentialism.

We may find that in our own spirit it is not important to make sure other people recognize our altruism. Is it even possible to recognize altruism? Should we assume people's intentions, good or bad? Is it enough to know that someone, somewhere, is secretly feeding orphaned kittens?

What if we consider that altruism is also instinctual, fast? That compassionate empathy might feel like getting kicked or moved to do something. It's not calculated with planned dominos going, "if I save this person at this moment, I'll be rewarded or get that promotion." The act of compassion is done simply for the sake of experiencing the needs and emotions of another and acting instinctively to do something about the situation.

Questions for Reflection:

Can you remember a time you acted altruistically, or when someone did a kind act for you?

Consider acting altruistically next time you have the chance, without thinking too much about it. Try to be spontaneous and not plan the moment. How did you feel?

Why do we feel the need to be recognized for our good deeds?

9. Are You Suffering From Stagnant Behavior and Learned Helplessness?

"Learned helplessness is the giving-up reaction, the quitting response that follows from the belief that whatever you do doesn't matter."

–Arnold Schwarzenegger

It is tough to be resilient and a problem solver, for that is a path that is for the person that wants to hold themselves accountable, to become the best version of themselves. This is not an easy path. One may find it rare to find a naturally resilient person, as it is often a product of how we are raised and nurtured. To become a rubber ball that just bounces up when it gets dropped down takes coping skills, self-talk, and a problem-solving mentality.

At my friend Nessa's lowest point, she wondered if it would just be better to give in. Lean heavily into vices, be in toxic relationships, feel stuck, and do everything that fed into her insecurities and only satiated her symptoms for brief periods of time. It was easier to slip into the pain than to do something about it. Stagnation is also tricky for the person experiencing it because it veers into things like depression.

As for my friend Wendy, it was more difficult to be patient. Rather than a depressed and hopeless demeanor like Nessa's, my friends and I were met with Wendy's wrath and aggression. After the storm, we would be met with either regret or excuses, but no apologies and no accountability. Blame would be placed on the person who upset her or the person who "hurt" her.

Some empaths argue, "You know I can't just turn the empathy off. I'm cursed to be this way." This comes from empaths who perhaps have not tried the right kind of boundaries and shields. They have surrendered to the hopelessness and helplessness of never being in full control.

Emotional Management

A lot of people believe they can not control their emotions. There is, weirdly, some truth and some untruth to that. We can not control the feelings of pleasantness, unpleasantness, arousal, and calmness, according to Psychologist Lisa Feld Barrett (2017). What we can control is how we respond.

Your brain gets these important signals in the body, but it doesn't know for certain what's causing them. The brain has past experience with similar feelings, so it's guessing. This can be a tough truth for people that say they trust their gut or know their intuition, especially if trauma is disguising itself as intuition. We learned how to respond to stimuli and the actions through our parents, our society, our peers, or anyone who expresses an emotional reaction to something. Sometimes our system one thinking may lead you to an emotional response driven by fear, primal energy, and survival. System two is your rational or practical system, that still has the benefit of the doubt and is able to walk you through a response to a problem to solve rather than accuse.

Stagnant, or something more?

Some folks are systematically in poverty or blocked from the path to happiness and success by roadblocks in their country that appear lawful.

We need to consider why people get into the positions that they do. Unless we know someone intimately, it is not appropriate to diagnose the cause of a person's stagnancy. The only person's stagnant behavior we should be worrying about is our own, to focus on what is within our control, and what is not.

In the realm of close relationships, we may have had a partner, parent, or friend who used stagnation and helplessness as a form of narcissism but that feels apart from empathy. This ends up being generic brand, regular attention-seeking behavior, and it's hard sometimes to discern from an actually treatable chemical imbalance. I do think it also enters a realm of self-focus that it may draw in and consume energy, but folks with difficult empathic and martyr/savior complexes may be drawn to such people: people who need 'fixing' or become 'projects'. I can see a very intense dark empath encouraging stagnation. An actualized and happy person is harder to control or feed off of than a stagnated one. But that same element of stagnation could also be a matter of 'I am weak or defeated or need help' as a way to keep someone close. A dark empath could for instance take advantage of normal or healthy empathy by suggesting "if you don't help harm me you are not empathic and are selfish".

I once had a cousin who was being kept overweight by an insecure partner. Them both being stagnant and overweight made him feel secure in that she would not leave him. When she would exercise, he would instantly sabotage her efforts and feed her junk food. He once openly admitted the worry of her being too attractive or thin would make her leave. This also removed a lot of accountability for him, because it was in truth his poor behavior and lack of faithfulness that ruined the relationship in the end.

Genuine stagnation is something that needs addressing but may attract a malignant empath. The reverse may be true- a malignant person may attract and 'capture' a genuine empath in their own need to be kind and non-judgemental.

How Energy Vampires Respond to Helplessness

An energy vampire would be really on board with a person who is either stagnant, helpless, or forced into the type of escapism that exhausts or disorients them, making them dependent on the vampire. I would say energy vampires could either prevent people from escapism without being involved or centered due to their own narcissism, or use escapism chronically themselves and require others to sink energy and time and resources in their own interest/escapist element. I see the latter a lot in people who think drinking is an important part of social behavior.

Feeling helpless allows someone else to pull your strings and give you false hope that makes you malleable and easy to manipulate. If we can find ways to be problem solvers, reflectors, and introspective, we can find ways to move forward without feeling stuck.

Questions for Reflection:

1. What kinds of peer pressure and socially learned helplessness might you stop partaking in?
2. When you feel stuck on a project or in life, what is something low-stakes you can do that allows for a quick dopamine boost to feel accomplished?
3. In your journal, list ten or more small things in your life that you can change, no matter how depressed, stagnant, or helpless you feel.

10. Don't Confuse Self Care With Escapism

"Almost everything will work again if you unplug it for a few minutes, including you."

— Anne Lamott

It should be no surprise that empathy and being an Empath are exhausting. It can be tiring on the spiritual, mental, physical, and emotional levels. Escapism is a thing that many humans turn to, and an empath is no exception. If one has had a long day of putting out emotional fires and saving depressive cats in trees, they are likely to want a long shower or a nice movie and popcorn night. Or maybe a glass of wine. Or spending time with their favorite no-drama person.

While some escapism can be healthy, it is important to put a time limit on it. Recharging your social battery can feel good, but there is a difference between binge-watching a season of Once Upon a Time in a night and not emerging from your room for five days. There is a difference between participating in your own well-being and refusing to participate at all.

When we choose to "escape" in one aspect of life that is often recreational, we often do this because another aspect of our life is causing us stress. It might be a relationship, work, a chore, or a situation.

Escapism is a singular action that doesn't include yourself. Self-care requires participating in yourself, in your environment, and in your life. Escapism often rejects everything except one activity or feeling, or rejects everything. Escapism often means escaping yourself as well, and you cannot heal something you are ignoring.

Some escapism can be healthy. If you go to an amusement park for the day, or camping, or go for a hike with friends to forget about work, I cannot blame you. From an ethical and health standpoint, it is not right to expect people to have their mind on work all the time. To reset the brain from the mundane is to prevent burnout.

This chapter contains clarification on which self-care tactics are more equivalent to escapism traps. Cheap escapism is a quick fix to symptoms of stress but may lead to negative feedback loops. These loops can lead to losing resources, with perpetual paths back into being broke financially, stressed, or burned out again. Effective self-care will help to form good habits, recognize limits, and regulate your mental health.

Retail Therapy

Should you buy cozy slippers or expensive shoes? Is it better to purchase a gadget to make prepping meals easier, or to buy a fancy decorative painting? One of my former addictions was to office supplies. Silly, I know.

Not all purchases have to be practical; it's nice to own a cute knicknack or a sentimental item. Sometimes buying things is an attempt to fill a void that needs to be addressed.

Swiping the card or adding to the cart does not necessarily fill a void. If we are having financial issues, acting like money is not an issue is the last way we want to act.

The spontaneity of shopping is what seems to elevate folks into better moods. It's unplanned and not the thing that is stressing you out. Even though you felt stress-free and carefree at the moment, your wallet and your regret are going to wake up pretty quickly. Folks with debt know they do not wish to go deeper.

Drugs, Medicine, Nutrients, and Healing practices

Disclaimer: The author is not qualified to give medical advice, and this is more something to reflect on than to take as advice.

When people want to feel in control or are untrusting of authorities like pharmacies and the health industry, which, in certain countries, is fair. The pricing on some medicine is downright criminal...

What is interesting is that when folks try to escape from tried and true medicine, they may be racking up a more expensive hospital bill when they dabble in homeopathy or botany.

Taking that daily medicine or vitamin can be great, but out of fear of spending too much on life-saving medicine, folks sometimes take alternative paths with healing their body that may not be great if they do not know what amounts their body is sympatico with. Pharmacists know the dosage based on some pretty exact science. Extracting pain relief properties from willow bark would be more expensive for your labour and time than just picking up a bottle of aspirin from the store. Working with belladonna, hallucinogens, or any chemical that is highly concentrated even in microdoses can be incredibly dangerous if not supervised or facilitated by a professional.

Cannabis is another tricky plant. The side effects and ways it treats the human psyche can be really inconsistent since dosage can be extremely different for different brains and bodies.

Addicts can lead others into escapism with peer pressure. They drink to escape. If you don't drink to escape with them, they feel something is wrong with you. It becomes a continuous conflict or the other person is pressured into participating in social drinking or drug consumption.

Venting vs Gossip

Venting is usually more centered around the frustrations over a situation, and gossip is more focused on the shortcomings of a person or persons. When I hear someone talking about another person in the form of gossip, there is a certain tenor about it that also makes me fear that I am also being talked about. If Joanie says, "I'm worried that Prue might not be doing her share of the work." has an entirely different tone than "Prue is definitely not working because she's always on the phone." Venting is a matter of putting something into words in order to feel it properly, and hopefully so someone hears and witnesses it.

Gossiping is sharing information, often as fact, because gossip is said by someone who already found the words. They aren't concerned about working through their feelings, and instead often have formed judgments that they are ready to spread to others. This can be especially dangerous if there is an unknown context. What is the reason that Prue is on the phone, is it because she is working out home-health care for her mother, or trying to find a babysitter for her child because she had to work late?

Exercise and Diet

Your relationship with your food and your self-esteem can play a large part in self-care vs escapism. A self-care act regarding food would feel closer to drinking tea that is good for you, or having a small comfort food like a macron to give you a tiny bit of joy. Escapism, however, would be drowning in your own sorrows in a sea of empty chip bags, take out meals, and some ice cream or alcohol.

Different eating disorders are often a kind of escapism into feeling in control of our diet, especially when the rest of the world feels out of control. Orthorexia is one form not talked often about, in which the affected person becomes obsessed with their health, eating, and exercise routine, to the point where this excessive preoccupation takes over their life (McLaren).

Exercise can be self-care, but we should not punish ourselves for the day we miss working out or the day we maybe put in half-effort at the gym. Punishing the psyche for not being in a good habit is akin to a bad habit, for it does not reenforce one's capability. There becomes a defeatist or self-pitying element that could feed into an unhealthy pattern. "If I can't do the whole workout, what's the point of it?" Becomes an excuse in its own right.

Movies and Television Shows

Having a group outing can have some great prosocial and bonding moments. What better way to share in a common interest or fandom than going to a movie?

Then there is the binge-watching of multiple seasons. Neglecting chores, work, commitments, and so on. This may be okay for one day, as everyone deserves a day off. Movies and television are yet another example of things being in moderation.

To bring a little bit of self-care back into media consumption, consider joining groups or calling someone to discuss what you are watching. Make some time to reflect on the show, daydream, or read up cool trivia on the making of the film. It might also be better to watch something inspiring rather than depressing, which is why you should be in touch with your mood and needs so that they are ignored by watching something, not in your universe.

Gaming

People from older generations seem to think video gaming is a worse form of escapism than watching a film or show, but video gaming, when used correctly, can both be excellent self-care, and on the flip side, be an addiction. Escapist gamers are expected to experience a time drain, money drain, and fall out of touch with friendships and family. They will lose touch with reality, eating quick snacks and consuming energy drinks. Their physical activity will lessen, their lack of Vitamin D from the sun will feed into their depression.

There is a healthier side to gaming. Social gamers make friends as they game. They find meetups and have specific times they meet that are not five-hour campaigns. They utilize important mental skills like problem-solving together, understanding physics, managing resources, and completing a goal together. It may not seem like anything but lights and gimmicks at face value, but folks that do not experience the dopamine or endorphin rush of success in the physical world, like to feel that sense of accomplishment among the pixels.

Even folks who treat video games socially can have a severe addiction. MMORPGs are a big part of creating in-depth realities and worlds. Existing in the virtual world for too long can lead to social anxiety in a reaction. Operating in a delusion that contains meaningful interaction may cause one to not function in social situations outside of gameplay, for our world no longer appears safe or accepted due to the addict's world. They get to exist meaningfully, in their perception, in a reality that means that there is no value in real life.

Games allow for a space without threat or consequences. This can be both beneficial and problematic. Folks who want to act negatively, troll, or say awful things will do so because they are anonymous, and this empowers and protects them.

The reality of a video game transplants reality for some, especially those who have experienced otherness, bullying, or very isolating situations in the "real", corporeal world.

The board gaming and tabletop role-playing games are also making a resurgence. The amount of make-believe and mutual acceptance of rules makes for yet another avenue for group problem solving, collaboration, and optimizing strengths and resources.

Gaming is also intergenerational. Games present a set of rules and realities that are agreed on, so people of many backgrounds are given a common language: the game itself. As long as you can take the time to learn it, you can translate across any barrier. Multiple age groups have reported the feelings of belonging and acceptance in role-playing groups, as they sometimes operate like a second family or a team.

Serial Dating

Sometimes one may be feeling lonely and stressed so you date without focusing on yourself. Throughout the relationship, you find yourself absorbing the other person's energy or personal baggage. You get bored, or stressed or worried. You have conflict and arguments without communicating or participating in problem-solving together. You break up, and, without examining what did not work or how you operated, you jump into the next relationship. The escapism of this nature leads to co-dependency, and not truly knowing what the self is like when left to your own devices.

Destination Addiction and Traveling

Destination addiction is when the thing that makes you happy is the next thing, and then the next thing. Many young folks get caught in the trap and expectation of "I'll be happy when I get a job." " I'll be happy when I get a partner." "I'll be happy when I get married." " I'll be happy when I have children." "I'll be happy when I have a house that I can call mine." These are all wonderful goals, but they should not be tied to happiness. One should not only be able to be happy in the present, but also should recognize that the destination is not as important as living in the now.

Some folks more literally have destination addiction, constantly picking up what little they have and doing cross-country trips. A friend of mine used to tell me that her "toxic trait" was whenever she felt like she wanted to leave her hometown or a job, she started daydreaming and making plans and itineraries… sometimes getting really close to pressing the "check out" or "purchase tickets" button.

Granted that she never acted upon this, I would say an online travel window-shopping adventure is not a bad thing, but the important part might be for one to reflect and figure out what it is that makes them want to run. Do they want to move somewhere else? Is there a problem they would rather not put up with or face? What if they were to confront that same problem in another state or country, would they move again?

CBT

CBT can be helpful for both empaths and energy vampires, particularly for those with PTSD or BPD. Throughout life, we learn patterns of thinking that are unhelpful and assumptive. A way of coping and undoing these patterns of thinking will allow for more appropriate and civil reactions to conflict. This starts with learning about one's biases due to trauma, as well as learning what motivates others. CBT allows one to be a problem solver rather than a complainer and gives one the capacity and accountability to change themselves, rather than giving into learned helplessness.

Cognitive-behavioral therapy (CBT) helps you to navigate your thoughts by changing the way you think and behave. It helps to take your negative thoughts and feelings that may put you in a feedback loop, and break them down into smaller elements to handle. Practices like self-talk and asking yourself questions help you reroute feeling overwhelmed, stressed, insecure, etc. It is not meant to rework you through past issues, but rather to give you coping mechanisms for you to deal with thoughts in the present.

You may be asked to analyze your thoughts to recognize if what you are thinking is unhelpful. For example, is your friend not texting you back because they are mad at you, or is there something else that might be occupying their time? Is there anything recently that you may have done to upset them? Is it helpful to let this worry fill your day? Is there an opportunity to let it go? Can you give yourself a few days and text them again?

CBT should be facilitated by a licensed professional, but there are manuals and literature that explain in depth how it works.

Therapy and Self Care

Self-care is not just reactive to stress, it is also proactive and preventative. Being able to self-talk with your brain allows for better self-control, and responding to people mindfully. Sometimes we can let our System 1 thinking (the gut reaction) overtakes our System 2 thinking (the reasonable and logical reaction) because it might be powered by trauma or instinct that has mistaken itself for intuition. These next two techniques, CBT and NLP, give strategies to slow the brain down from being distrustful or hyper-reactive to a perhaps mundane and straightforward situation.

NLP

NLP or neuro-linguistic programming, can give you tools for both preventative measures and treating symptoms in response to anxiety, an energy vampire attack, trauma, insecurity, etc. The practice of NLP is to help one decode and encode their brain, and understand their own personal language in their thoughts.

While it does not have as much scientific backing as CBT, there have been accounts of its success. It is also important to have someone trained in NLP to coach you for a few sessions, rather than going through a self-taught process, which will not be as effective. Many feel that NLP is better left in communication technique until it can get more evidence in being helpful in the field of psychotherapy.

NLP uses four pillars in its techniques, with one pillar called Anchoring. Anchoring, or sensory awareness, involves turning pressure points, squeezes, pokes, or tapping in order to bring about specific emotional states. Another pillar is known as Rapport. Value is placed on having trust with others and building relationships with other people. A third pillar is Outcome Thinking, which is rerouting a negative thinking path and bringing it to a goal or outcome-oriented thought process, rather than a negative spiral. This leads us to our fourth pillar: Behavior Flexibility, in which one has a fresh perspective and consents to being okay with doing things differently in order to make informed choices.

NLP allows for reflection, and examination of one's negative thoughts and feelings. Often, practitioners will use a meditation or mind-palace exercise to tour one's thoughts in a safe way. This allows for becoming a better communicator in expressing one's needs or in drawing a boundary, or having an all round fair, and stress free conversation.

Do you Deserve Peace?

Energy vampires and narcissists are concerned with centering themselves at all times. Those of us who feel undeserving of self-care should remember that others do not even hesitate for a moment in what they deserve.

In some cases, a person engaging in escapism without an energy vampire or narcissist will likely interfere with the toxic person's sense of control. It was not their idea, and probably was not their idea of escapism. As much as you deserve self-care, you also deserve the right to say no to an activity that makes you uncomfortable.

Questions for Reflection:

What is a form of escapism you participate in that can be changed to a form of self-care?

If you do something excessive, is there a way to do that thing in moderation?

Use at least one of the self-care techniques from this chapter. How did it go? Does it work for you? If not, why?

11. Self-Love Languages

"We can never obtain peace in the outer world until we make peace with ourselves."

—The Dalai Lama

Self-care is important for empaths, especially empaths at risk of burnout, or becoming a dark empath.

We may have heard the "you can't pour from an empty cup" or the "put on your own oxygen mask" deal a million times, but it's true! I have friends who have found themselves in situations where they really did want to help others but had let all their commitments and obligations fill up their time and energy, leaving them with emotional, spiritual, mental, and physical fatigue.

The Five Love Languages has gained popularity over the years for partners, but I would like to take the time to propose the love languages for the self and for friendships. This list is not exhaustive. Many of the self-care languages can also intermingle with each other. Some can be done daily, some are best arranged and paired with other forms of self-care.

Time for the Self /Change of Pace:

For many, this defaults to baths, showers, pedicures, etc. There is probably a broader definition: Anything that centers your body. You may prefer wrapping yourself in a blanket like a burrito. Participating in someone else's pace or their change of pace. There are low stakes things you can do.

The empathic and anxious brain needs a break from the mundane. Saying yes, getting out of the house, and letting someone else trustworthy drive the bus for a bit is a good way to consent to a safe surprise or adventure. Surrendering control of an activity can also be a huge relief for folks that have to lead and make active choices all the time. Spontaneity and adventure, or not having a plan means actively participating in the journey and not having to overthink each itinerary or event.

During your time for you, re-engage in an old hobby or personal project. When was the last time you worked on your novel, painting, or play?

Sensory:

Many sensitives, intuitives, and neurodivergent folk really get into sensory experiences to feel a sense of calm. Some people feel better in the presence of water, like taking a shower or washing dishes. Youtube has a plethora of ASMR videos, as well as other videos with sounds that either engage or calm the brain. You can additionally find videos with binaural beats, lo-fi music, meditation music, isochronic tones, or many other music genres that give positive goose bumps to the brain. I like to call them "brain fuzzies".

Many folks have taken to purchasing weighted blankets. Grounding in this way is helpful for empaths and sensitive people. The deep pressure causes the physical body to feel more at ease, and allows the spiritual body to cocoon and recharge.

Writing:

Journalism, social media. Remember what we said about gossip? Many people who vaguebook are also participating in a kind of gossip that removes them from the accountability of their assumptions. In a maybe kind way they are trying not to identify a person, but may also be manipulative in the sense that they hope the unnamed person realizes it is them.

Breathing/Meditation:

This is tough for those that do not know how to sit still, and that is perfectly okay. In the spirit of inclusiveness, not everyone has to meditate while in a seated lotus. You can meditate walking, washing dishes, or before bed. Meditation is meant to maintain focus on the breathing and the moment. You do not need an empty mind or even to really pay attention. If your mind wanders, acknowledge the thought quickly, and then turn back to neutral.

Your environment:

Change your environment short term or long term. Make a blanket fort. Redecorate a room or clean it more thoroughly then you ever have. It also might be a good time to get organized; cluttered rooms tend to reflect a cluttered mind. Why do you think girls get that reputation of "she got a tattoo, changed her hair, moved out, and rearranged her furniture? Clearly, she's goin g through a lot right now." Regularly finding homes away from home: cafes, libraries, movie theaters, if considered safe spaces, will allow for comfortable existence and a change in scenery without being too expensive.

Micro changes in your environment can be helpful, like Vitamin D, a sun lamp, temperature, bulletin boards, and decorations. Cleaning one floor or handling one stack of papers chips away at a larger mountain. Consider having a special blanket and book somewhere for cozy alone time.

For focus, Lo-fi has become very popular, particularly over the pandemic. Many office workers, freelancers, and other remote workers found this for the need of some kind of ambient noise to replace the buzz of the office space.

Accepting Help:

Asking for help can be one of the bravest things you can do. Demanding or expecting it is not, because it has not been communicated kindly or effectively. It's better to ask early, and not when it becomes a crisis. The sooner you ask for help, the less energy consumption you will experience over worry and anxiety. There will also be less fall out between yourself and the other people it involves. Give someone the opportunity to say no or set a boundary. Waiting to ask for help when at the last moment puts people in a bind because they feel like they have no choice but to help.

Questions for Reflection:

What is your self-love language? If you have more than one, list those too.

What is something you can tell yourself every day to keep your perspective on self-love and to convince yourself that you deserve it?

Try one of the love languages out on yourself and then reflect in your journal on the results.

12. The Love Languages of Partner and Friendship

"It's all about falling in love with yourself and sharing that love with someone who appreciates you, rather than looking for love to compensate for a self-love deficit."

— *Eartha Kitt*

It is an act of self-care to actively participate in our friendships, as long as it is an act of love, without the expectation of reciprocation or some kind of transaction. We may sometimes forget that giving time and energy to relationships allows us to strengthen connections. It takes a village or community to keep each other sane and healthy. Those in whom you invest your time when you are at your best will remember you for it. This does not mean that you should trip over yourself or deteriorate your health to make someone happy, but people like to feel loved and appreciated. It also does not help to ask someone for quality time or any other act of love if you have never shown any kind of love, kindness, or acts of care for them. It does not seem fair.

To form this bond of trust in communicating, a friendship cannot only have boundaries and stop signs. To keep the balance, one ought to find opportunities for green lights too. Here are some ways to show, receive, or give love and care.

Physical Closeness:

Some folks connect well via touch. Pressure, poking, tapping, sex, cuddling. It is important to communicate what kinds of physical closeness work for you, which ones make you uncomfortable, and which ones bring you the most joy.

Be warned if your partner has narcissistic traits and uses physical closeness as a tactic for manipulation. People who value physical closeness value this for connection, not just for sex or for pleasure. Intimacy can be cuddles, skin-to-skin contact, dancing, or sleeping in the same bed. A person who centers their needs around sex may be experiencing some insecurities or something deeper that they need to work out with a therapist.

Proximity/Body Doubling:

If you remember in the Self-love section, we discussed setting aside time for yourself. It is possible to do this through another person. As a species, we are very social creatures. It is important to be reminded that we are human if another human is in the room. Working or existing on our own can lead to distractions, zoning out, dissociative behaviors, and a general sense of un-grounding. Another person around puts you back in your body.

A friend or family member could be working on a project or chore while you work on your computer, or you can both work on painting something. If you are needing someone around while you get a task done that you do not wish to do, they could play a video game with their headphones connected.

This particular self-care and friendship practice makes it difficult for those that want to cry out their own self-sacrifice and martyrdom. Often, these dark empaths are over-centering someone to gain purpose. But if one is doing something because they want to do it, they can not pretend it's about the other person. One can unabashedly be upfront without weaving it through someone else's needs.

Words of Affirmation:

This does not mean one is fishing for compliments. Words of affirmation means words that support, uplift, and empathize with another person in a positive manner that further supports or confirms the relationship. It can be something like, "I love when you do _____," or, "It means a lot when you ____." You can vocalize a good memory to your best friend. You can say you trust your partner or are grateful for them. You can tell someone you're grateful for them or madly in love with them. As long as you genuinely mean it, it is affirming.

Deep Interactions:

These can vary between meaningful academic conversations, spiritually common conversations, moments of vulnerability, and storytelling.

Deep interactions may be primarily vulnerable and resource-consuming, and fundamentally 'unusual'. We don't do them every day, we do them when they matter and mean something. A lot of tough relationships make them the only interaction and do them constantly (treating a friend as a therapist, e.g.), or not at all (too many walls, fear of judgment, etc).

Deep interactions could also include Witnessing. The friend who is there when you get the call that someone died, and is the first person to help you with breaking the news, just by being present. Or someone who comes to visit a grave or sits with you outside a hospital room. The person who drove you to the birth of your child. Someone who, somewhat through chance, was there for an irreplaceable moment, and treated it respectfully.

Relatable Interactions:

These include memes, texting, comedy shows, geeking or nerding out over a fandom, hobby, or activity. Those "oh my gosh, me too!" moments.

Acts of Service/Quality time/Gifts:

These three are put in the same category due to the fact that they all involve one's time and resources. You are giving your quality time, your skill, services, and money to a loved one to show them you care. Gifts should be meaningful, and they do not have to be material. What is a gift? A gift can be something that you know someone needs. A gift can be a person, specifically a person spending time with you. Quality time can involve travel and adventures. Acts of service might take time away from children or work, but you know the gift of your time means a lot to your person. This is why I feel there is often a cross-pollination or even a blurred meaning between acts of service, quality time, and gifts.

What does it mean when these love languages are weaponized by others? Or when they are not radically accepted by both parties?

A person who makes fun of another person's hobbies can lead to a disconnect in enthusiasm or authenticity in the relationship. My friend, Billy, who broke up recently with his girlfriend, confessed, "I feel like I could not be myself in front of her, she would only laugh at my interests." This was usually when Billy participated in video games or painted miniature figures.

Billy would engage in his version of escapism without his girlfriend. Later, Billy dated someone different, Camilla, who engaged in her own escapism in a body-doubling way. When Billy painted, Camilla might read a book quietly. When Billy played video games, Camilla would support the escapism directly by encouraging it.

There is a therapist who has a wonderful method of gamifying couples therapy with love languages. As an activity for two people that want to realize how they authentically care for the other, they can try the following experiment:

Write down, or say to a mediator or therapist, one good thing that you will do for each other in the next week, and then see if you can each guess what that one thing was. The goal is to both do the good thing, and for it to not be noticed. This will not just encourage any two people to do one more good thing (even though perhaps for the wrong reason - competition), but the process of guessing what that thing was can become very complicated. Now paying attention, both people may find themselves noticing a massive amount of small good things that they do for each other and that the 'one good thing' they planned is impossible to detect among all the good things that were forgotten or so far ignored. This alternatively could just highlight a different truth- there are no natural 'good things', and that may signal a relationship that should come to its end.

Questions for Reflection:

How can you better communicate your needs and love language preferences to your friends and/or partner?

What are some love languages that your friend/partner has that you find uncomfortable? How can you have a mature conversation about it?

What is an activity you can do with a friend between now and next week? Reflect in your journal on how it goes.

13. Protecting Yourself and Setting Healthy Boundaries

"The only people who get upset about you setting boundaries are the ones who were benefiting from you having none."

—Unknown

Empathy without boundaries allows for a synthesis of one's own feelings and other's feelings crashing like waves into each other. A person who constantly allows the emotions of others to wash over them will experience and sit in these feelings, and be filled with such sorrow and distress that they will begin to feel like a victim. "When we're enmeshed with other people and we can't differentiate between their feelings and our own, we'll often fall into unconscious caretaking behaviors (McClaren)."

Many folks seem to think that acting on empathy involves sacrifice or abandonment of the self. This is simply not the case; true empathy allows for self-care and prioritizing your needs as well as those of others. People who do not divulge their boundaries can be depressed or devalued, feeling that their needs are not important. Alternatively, some people hide their boundaries or invent them when it is convenient, so that they can play a victim card for a transgression later on.

It is additionally not fair of us to identify close friends as energy vampires, narcissists, or dark empaths, if we have not given them a fair shot at establishing boundaries or letting them know what we like and dislike. Even the best people are not mind readers. Occasionally, an acquaintance has the misfortune of poking the right button. Are they a narcissist or have you just not gotten to know them? Furthermore, just because someone does not fit into your life doesn't mean that they are bad or an energy vampire. I love chatty friends, but some of my introverted friends do not. They politely just add time limits to when they visit their outgoing, loud buddies. There is a difference between friendship chemistry, and a person who is plainly toxic.

Defining and expressing your needs, and being able to assert them is a huge form of protection for empaths (Orloff, Kripalu). This allows you to remember your worth and to remember if something does not feel right in a relationship.

Sometimes you can not verbally set boundaries, because the other party is not up for communication with dignity. In this chapter, you will find a few ways to protect yourself as an empath.

Shielding:

There are a few ways to shield yourself from others so that you do not take on their energy so easily. You can do this before you leave the house for the work day. You can also step away for a minute if you realize you may be going into a potentially draining situation.

There are a variety of visualizations out there that you can learn, but here we will highlight two, specifically the Golden Case Exercise and the Screen Door Technique.

For the Golden Case, close your eyes. Imagine a white or yellow light above you, and another below you. This light spreads wide on either side of you, encompassing you like a plant under a bell jar. Imagine this light as an impenetrable shield. The light begins to glow into a translucent gold. It is made of love, life, and an intention for your highest good.

Grounding:

Empaths love nature. The earth is always ebbing, flowing, healing, and changing in such a natural way that is both complex and just *is*. Remind yourself of what it is to *be* by taking a walk or meditating seated on a large rock. You can also stand and try letting your feet touch loamy dirt or nice soft grass and feel the earth's healing energy through your feet (Orloff).

If you do not have access to the outside due to your job or living situation, you can do a visualization where you imagine yourself becoming a tree. Put on some soft music or nature sounds. Stand up and close your eyes. Imagine roots coming out of your toes and reaching deep into the ground. Feel your skin thicken and yet breathe everywhere. You become taller and taller, at least three times as tall as you are now. You feel branches and twigs beginning to spread from your fingers, arms, shoulders, and head. As your leaves grow, you feel them flapping in the wind as a soft breeze flows by. When you are ready to stop, reverse the process. Feel the leaves recede back into the twigs and branches. Feel the branches shrink back near your body. As you become shorter, and the roots below your feet disappear, you take a deep breath, and remember being at peace with nature for a small but sacred amount of time.

Cleansing:

It is good for the soul and body to shower both physically and spiritually. Use a cleansing visualization exercise when you are getting back from a particularly long day with multiple interactions with draining people, or one very draining person.

Energy vampires often carry malignant or stagnant energy that is, in a sense, contagious and can rub off on you. You can wipe or scrub this off via intention in your visualization. Imagine a shower of sparkling, healing energy is streaming down your body. Perhaps it is a calm blue, a healing green, or a perfect shade of purple with silver glitter. As it pours, imagine each place that your hand goes over is being washed or drained away of whatever energetic clog, grime, or dirt was there before.

193

Knowing your Inner Child:

Your relationship with your inner child can either be your greatest strength or your greatest vulnerability. If you give a narcissist the option to exploit it, it may be your downfall.

People who had troubling, complicated, or turbulent childhoods may allow themselves to be energetically held by narcissists, energy vampires, or dark empaths. It may be helpful to remind them that a person like that should not fill the void of what they could not get before. If you are experiencing this yourself, you may wish to forgive your inner child, and tell them that everything will work out in the end.

To know that inner child, is to remember the willingness to find fun and find meaning in things without letting rules and cultural norms dictate harmless play. Energy vampires sometimes do not like to witness a person experiencing joy if they are drowning in their own negativity.

Energy vampires can easily push against politeness and use it to force negative or draining conversations. Energy vampires demand attention and problem solving, or just wear you down in general. The inner child does not put up with that. Your inner child would not stand and listen politely to a person's ranting and ravings. They would go, "Bored now!" and move on to their next activity. Or they might say, "'I want to do something else," and walk away. While it would be hilarious for you as an adult to say those statements, it is not ideal and has consequences. The point is, the inner child has boundaries, says things simply, and knows when something feels wrong. Adults are prone to worrying about their reputation, about what is polite or proper, and the idea that being patient is more important than self-care. Connecting with your inner child reminds you that those social norms can trap you in conversations and relationships that do not have your mental health or best interests at heart.

For example, I once let a coworker at a job complain about something going on in their personal life. I had a lot of paperwork due that evening. Rather than ask her if we could carry out the conversation on a later date, I really wanted to be a good friend to her, and let her carry on. She was not an energy vampire, but she was very much consuming my energetic resources, and my time. Since she may not have been aware of my level of business, I should have informed her of my workload.

It is important to note here that protecting yourself empathetically and energetically is not only important for extreme cases, like energy vampires. Normal, everyday situations with people can be quite draining on their own.

Setting boundaries with coworkers can help with future conversations. A friend of mine, Jaida, was a worker at a non-profit. They approached when I stepped out of a meeting for a moment. They began talking and Rambling. Jaida calmly but firmly stated, "I need to get back to work," with no pleasantries attached. At first, she was quite taken aback. Jaida thought she had offended the coworker. She was taken aback at the moment, but later in the day informed Jaida what she did was the right thing: "Sorry, I realized I ambushed you when I was bored."

From that moment on, it actually fixed a bit of the intrusive banter that she and Jaida had engaged in in the workplace. My friend ended up being very glad that she did not try to play by the social rules or dress it up with pleasantries.

Responding:

There are a few ways to respond to an overwhelming situation. You can stand twenty feet away from the suspected source. Wait about two to five minutes and see if you can tell the difference.

If physical separation is not possible, count to ten. It may seem cliche, but sometimes it is helpful to think of a different place that is much more peaceful and delightful than the current scenario.

If your response involves a conversation, practice the pause. Give your brain 3-5 seconds to really think about how you will reply to the person. This can save you from conflict, and be a good strategy to realize if a person genuinely wants to hear your opinion, or if they are trying to get a rise out of you.

Favorite person and Hyperfixations:

It can be really difficult to see through the rose-colored glasses that we might put on accidentally or on purpose. Sometimes we can like a person so much that any redflags can be justified as either a yellow flag, or something we convince ourselves that will most assuredly change later.

Compassion:

Compassion is a tool that helps us to be empathetic without being a fixer. The ability or awareness of being an empath does not endow us with the obligation to pick up other people's pain or to make their suffering less. Many folks think that compassion always involves immediate action, or dropping what you are doing, or engaging in some kind of sacrifice. Being compassionate can involve acknowledgement, a plan for listening, or simply holding space for someone.

Buttons and Your Emotional Remote Control

Who has access to your emotional remote control? When someone finds a button, there are ways to take back your power.

For a person who says you're fat, do not get in a conversation with them about dieting choices or what you are doing to be healthier. Change the topic, or tell them you are quite content as you are. Even if you have insecurities about your weight, they do not have a right to that knowledge, especially if they are going to be critical. Do not let them have access to this button. You have bodily autonomy, not them.

For a person who says you need to do more or accomplish more, they are hitting the achievement button of your remote with their version of success. You do not need to justify your version of success. Simply tell them you are doing the best you can with what is available, whether it is resources, effort, money, or time.

For the energy vampire that says you would look better if you had just a little more makeup, tell them how the right person you date will not care whether you have make up or not. In modern society, professionalism is not determined by how much makeup you wear.

Is Empathy always deserved by others?

In an ideal world, yes. Everyone deserves empathy, but not everyone deserves action and affirmation based on Empathy. Active empathy can contribute to victim mindsets, burn out, or people taking advantage of you.

Sacred Space

Additionally, it will help you to have spaces or at least one place where you can always be yourself.

Some examples are a writer's cottage, a place in the wilderness, a special room in the house. Some more digitally inclined folks like to have community spaces on Discord or special interest websites and apps. A place to be authentic and genuine is ultimately fulfilling for the soul.

Dunbar's Number

Some psychological theories suggest that we are not able to maintain more than a certain amount of relationships with others. Anthropologist Robin Dunbar figured that humans can only maintain 150 meaningful connections, give or take, at a time. Anything over 150 may be a mix of acquaintances or people that you can at the very least identify by name or face, and maybe know an interesting nugget about (BBC.com). These limitations are due to the fact that the human brain can only hold so much in terms of how many people you can care about. Even in a sociological sense, 150 seemed to also be the number of how big a community or group of people can get before they end up dissolving or having multiple subgroups drop off. This held true when primates were observed grooming or partaking in social behavior (BBC.com).

We are also the average of the people we surround ourselves with, according to Jack Canfield, author of Chicken Soup for the Soul. Say you had 10 friends, and 7 of those friends were generally positive people. And only 3 were more negative or simply stuck/stagnant. You would probably have a more optimistic outlook than those who have the negative perception, because the average attitude of your group would influence your demeanor.

It's not that we don't care about other humans, it's that we are not equipped to handle multiple directions of emotions, energy, or communication threads. This may be helpful when our plate of people feels full, or our desire to be helpful feels capped at a certain number of projects. Keeping our limitations in mind, we may learn to say "no" more as a boundary when we are met with providing favors, volunteering, or having the capacity to listen to someone in a bad spot.

People living rent-free in your head

We can mentally evict them or treat them like an unwanted roommate, especially if this person is one of your inner critics or brain goblins, as in a figment of your imagination. Seriously though, people often live rent-free in our head, especially people who do not deserve it.

If a person is monopolizing your thoughts and bringing you distress, kindly tell them to move out. Imagine a goodbye party or ceremony. Ask the imagined version in your head to vacate the premises.

Family, Home, and Work

The three spaces a typical person often has to exist in require setting energetic boundaries, because you want to feel safe and grounded in order to make these places productive, cozy, inviting, or predictable. Say yes or no if you want to. Don't just put up with it.

Set limits to how often you can visit family. If you have toxic parents, tell them how often you can visit, or leave when it gets bad. You do not owe it to them, no matter how much they tell you, to exist in a space that is triggering or bad for your mental health.

The workplace can be empathetically and mentally overstimulating. There are noises, people who always need something. Keep strict office hours, or try to be friendly and assertive when someone comes to bother you at the wrong time.

There are some who will not respond well to your boundaries, it may not be in your best interest to show them why they are doing so. Sometimes it is in your best interests to walk away. We do not always owe someone an explanation for cutting ties, especially if we are certain that they would have an extreme reaction to that reasoning. Some people have behavior that is protection from some trauma or hurt that they learned worked for them. "For us to call that out when these dysfunctional patterns are 'working' for them is like taking away someone's security blanket when they are not ready to let it go." (Huynh & Simon)

It is important to know our worth, and to notice if a friend or partner is not putting in reciprocal energy. You don't have to sever ties but don't have to put in energy. Don't externalize your power. No one can control you without your permission.

Affirmations:

This list of affirmations is sorted based on your needs as an empath in a variety of mindsets and situations. You can say a single phrase 3 times, or pick 3 phrases to say once each day.

Burnout

I am doing what I can.

I am doing the best I can with the tools I am given

It is not shameful to make time for my needs.

I do not have to help everyone I meet.

Setting Boundaries

It is okay for me to not help everyone who needs help.

I need to wear my oxygen mask before I put someone else's on.

Avoiding Martyrdom/Judgment

The way other people carry out their actions or duties is not within my control, and that is okay.

People heal when they choose to heal

It is not my responsibility to heal others or force growth at my preferred rate.

I can feel the gratitude of a person without words of affirmation. The universe recognizes my efforts.

Self-Care

I give myself permission to fill or maintain my cup.

Recognizing One's Own Emotions vs Absorbing Others'

I do not have to experience pain on behalf of another person

My vessel carries my beautiful emotions.

My vessel knows its limits.

I can be compassionate without sacrificing my health

Return to sender /Return to the source (It especially helps to say either of these affirmations three times in order for emotions you may have absorbed to return to the person who gave them to you either accidentally or maliciously).

Verbal and Physical Boundaries

You are under no obligation to hug others. You may not want energy to transfer to you from them, or you simply may just not want to hug someone that day.

Control how much time you spend listening to a person who may try to fill your space with chatter or their general social needs. "No" is a complete sentence.

It's okay to tell someone, "I'm sorry, I'm not up for going to a party tonight," or "Let's discuss this when you're calmer. I can't tolerate yelling," or "I need to meditate and be quiet right now," or "I can't talk more than a few minutes unless you want to discuss solutions." Sometimes changing communication patterns with friends is a retraining process, but being consistent with setting kind but firm limits will protect you from energy vampires.

Digital Health

It is important to be informed, as well as make sure what news you are reading is accurate. It is also a necessity to your health to not take in multiple tragedies and further research them so that you're spiraling emotionally.

Particularly during the Covid-19 Pandemic, more and more folks were exposed and bombarded with a plethora of tragedies, economic crises, and the like. If absorbing this information through social media platforms like Facebook, this can lead to a rather dissociative activity known as "doom scrolling." Doom scrolling puts the phone or computer user into a state of worry, hopelessness, helplessness, and depression. It can feel like the world or current situation will never get better.

Basic phone use can even be tricky. Have you ever already been bothered by something, and then someone texts you something pretty insignificant, but something about the message just sets you off? In your not best headspace, or even a good one, have you ever misread the tone of someone messaging you?

Take frequent breaks from your phone to reset your energy, even if your exposure has not been negative. It is good for your eyes and brain. As an empath, being overly connected to the global community can feel like you are trying to take on the world's stress and suffering on your own…which no one asked you to do.

Martyrs tend to help you remember the fact that they overextend themselves. We are living in a world where it is no longer socially or ethically acceptable to work yourself into the ground. We still, however, have folks that glamorize the grind and hard labor, especially on social media. Try to ignore these folks, as they are simply trying to engage in pain olympics, or feel proud about how fast they are working themselves to death.

Social media

Humans are less empathetic on social media because there's something in our primal brain that is not identifying whether we are communicating with another human being. Why do we talk to each other as though we are on a battleground?

What if we remembered that the folks typing out in their best command of the (typed) English language they can, are in fact tangible, corporeal people. We do not get to see their facial expressions, body language, or the tiniest micro expression that has its own language.

These folks typing their words are human beings who bleed, who have families, who love someone, who eat, who laugh, who want inner peace, who want to dance, or chill. They have flesh and similar humanoid shape. Are our mirror neurons unable to activate because we do not see another human being experiencing life?

What if, instead of associating what you're reading on a screen with a floating head with opinions and an attitude, what if you saw the person you were slinging insults at? You see a young person. They are in a purple long sleeve shirt, with rounded cheekbones and genuinely concerned eyes? With the bags under them. What if you noticed that they almost finished a mug of tea, and their skirt is being tugged on by a toddler while they type? Do you see their humanity? Did you know they sold their car today because they are struggling financially? Did you know their parents just died within a week and a half of each other? Would you perhaps have been more gentle with them in your comments? Did you know how much the person loves and misses their brothers in another state? Of course you don't, because on a social media platform, it is all too easy to deconstruct one's humanity, or isolate a single personality trait, and extrapolate the overall identity of a complex person.

What if we were aware that human beings exist as we do on the other side of this screen? Would we then be so poignant, condescending, brutal, or unforgiving?

What if we educated with compassion? Debated without sneering? And informed without condescension? What if we refused to believe every person has malicious or backhanded or nefarious intentions?

Questions for Reflection:

1. If you feel like you are not great at setting your own boundaries, is there a way to think about the boundaries you would ask another person to start using? Do you have a friend you wish would say no more? If a person lived with you and saw how you responded to others, what ideas might they have for you and your boundaries?
2. Is there a way to boundary-swap with a person you are close to, and try it out in a safe and healthy way? Find out at least one boundary, and tell them one of yours. See how it goes and reflect.
3. Try out at least one form of protection this week for energy vampires and narcissists. Reflect any changes in behavior or in energy in your journal.

14. Your Empathy Meter

There are ways to be in tune with your mind, spirit, and body before you hit burn out, or before you reach a decision that could lead to burnout. Being able to identify your energy level, mood, fatigue, are all very important tasks whether you are encountering people or not.

Spoon Theory

A trending phrase amongst some groups has fallen along the lines of "I don't have spoons for that." Spoon theory originated from a woman who wrote an essay on what it is like to have lupus. Christine Miserandino explained to her friend that when you are healthy, it can feel like you have unlimited spoons. When you have chronic illness, mental illness, or something that occupies you on a day to day basis, it can really affect the amount of energy you have (Miserandino). This has little to do with capability or time. It more or less deals with the amount of "spoons" you start with each day.

Let's say you have chronic depression or anxiety. It may cost a healthy person one spoon to get out of bed, but for you, it might take two or three. Perhaps you are already thinking about all the things you have to get done. Maybe you are dreading going into work, because you do not feel you will do well. People with chronic and mental illnesses start each day with a set number of metaphorical spoons, each one representing the physical and mental energy it takes to complete a daily task or social interaction. Smaller tasks, like showering or getting dressed, may cost only one spoon, while larger tasks, like cooking or vacuuming, may take three or four spoons. On days with increased pain or anxiety, what was once a simple task may require multiple spoons.

Some folks, even people with mental illnesses, have a spoon override. If they like to help people, it gives them an additional spoon or two if they feel capable of doing so. It is difficult for us to do something for ourselves; it may feel selfish or like we do not deserve to set aside more time for our needs. For our best friend or our romantic partner, or even a stranger on the street, we will drop what we are doing, because we want them to have a good day. Or, empathetically, we know what it is like to struggle, and do not want someone else to go through it. People who we have a true connection with someone will not experience a spoon cost or an energy cost. People on our frequency will not always fall into our empathy meter, for helping them is more fulfilling than anything we have ever experienced. This could be possible with a soulmate or a childhood best friend.

Thinking about it, I wonder how altruism and spoon theory might go hand in hand to a degree? Something to philosophize about in your own time.

Spoon theory helps everyone, but I know a lot of people with social anxiety who use it in their lexicon. A few of my socially anxious friends also happen to be empaths. A phone call to the doctor may take 2 or 3 spoons. A party or night to the club may use up all the remaining spoons they have. Some introverts I know have to take it easy the whole day just to be able to summon the spoons for any crowd.

It is possible to gain spoons back, but note that it takes time. You may need to engage in more recharging or self care. A nap, reading a book, or taking a vacation are only a few examples. I feel like many professors go on sabbatical as a way to recharge spoons. They ignore their needs for so long and then have to take a literal year just to get back to a sense of feeling like themselves again.

Spell Slots

Spoon theory has spread like hot cakes to multiple spaces. The D&D (Dungeons & Dragons) folks have, of course, come up with a metaphor that works for them, and may work for you. In a game of

D&D, characters can cast spells, and certain spells take a lot of power or focus. To keep track of how much energy it takes to cast spells, a character has 'spell slots', almost like metaphorical pockets that show how many spells can be done in a day. For each small spell, you need at least one small pocket, or spell slot, while large spells need large pockets. You may have many small pockets and one large pocket, so you have to be very careful about how you use your spells. But, in an emergency, you can always fit a small spell in a large pocket, but not vice-versa. This means you get to do the extra spell, but you lose the spot for the large one. And then, every night, all the spell slots (pockets) are emptied so you can start all over again.

This idea of spell slots has come up for describing emotional bandwidth, energy, and our ability to get-things-done. For example, if you are having a good day, you may have many spell slots, large and small, to fill with chores, helping your friends, or even to problem-solve a large crisis. But if you are grieving or under a lot of stress, you may have no large spell slots, and therefore can't quite fit 'large' problems, like a crisis happening to someone else. This isn't a thing to feel bad about- your large spell slots, or emotional pockets, are already full with something else, but running a quick errand or cooking yourself a good meal may be much smaller, and you have space for those things. In spaces that use this description, it is easy to say to someone 'I have large spell slots' is a good way to show not just a willingness to help, but the capacity to handle it even though it is large or complicated.

There are many different signs and signals that your body, mind, and spirit give you when you have reached empathy burnout, or feel unbalanced in life. These three lists below can be signs of your behavior and life happenings if you are in need of a change or may be letting other people's energy in too much.

Social Signs:

- Irritability
- Anxiety about interactions that are otherwise normal
- Your friends are asking more if something is wrong
- Feeling more withdrawn
- Going to more parties or shopping more
- Skepticism about information and reading into the things people tell you
- Trying to judge and predict people's future behaviors
- Taking offense more or getting defensive
- Reading into microexpressions more often
- Availability assumptions either way, of feeling like you cannot leave town because you may be needed, or assuming your friends are available if you need them
- Hobbies or things you once enjoyed no longer bring you joy
- Being out of touch with yourself and others

Physiological Signs:

Your body language and physique may change as follows:

- Slumping more
- Folding your arms when talking to people
- Easily overstimulated
- Tired/Fatigued
- Zoning out during a speech or conversation (when you normally would not)

Spiritual signs and/or Signs from the Universe:

- More perceived bad luck situations e.g. "Why me or Why does this always happen to me?"

- Asking the universe what lessons are you supposed to be learning?
- That you are trying to look for signs to the universe for change
- Finding patterns of negativity
- Animal crossings, seeing more of a certain kind of animal
- Feeling stuck
- The desire for change
- Feeling restless

Some of these listed items may seem contradictory. For instance, you may feel withdrawn, or you might party more if you are unbalanced. What counts is what is unusual for you personally, and what may be interfering with your life. Someone who does not normally party may be trying to get away from a specific obligation or responsibility. Someone who is normally extroverted but is now withdrawn may no longer feel safe in their social circles anymore due to a stalker.

Separating Emotions

Do you know whose emotions are whose? Here is a check-in survey of questions you can use to walk yourself through an emotional state in which the root of it may be unidentifiable:

Is there a reason I may be feeling this way? Did I come into contact recently with someone else's residual energy or extreme emotions? What should my emotion be at this point in the day? Do I have anything to look forward to in my day? When was the last time I ate or drank something?

Eating or drinking may seem silly, but it can be very grounding. Sometimes when our body needs something, like rest or nourishment, we act a bit more sensitive than necessary.

People who overwhelm you or take up too much of your time will leak into other parts of your day. You may find yourself thinking about them when they are not there. Their influence, commentary, and criticisms cause you to have imaginary conversations to anticipate outcomes. You are rehearsing a question that a healthy communicator would be able to handle without taking offense.

Second Chances and forgiveness are super important in maintaining empathy, but at what cost? A second chance can have a lot of hope and trust tied to why it happens in the first place. There is also the case, however, when the first chance is so brutally dishonored and awful, that no point can be reached of giving a second chance. You can also forgive and still have boundaries or even change your boundaries. People do not have to be on a fixed point in your friendship with them; it can ebb and flow as you see fit.

Whose feelings are whose? An important question to ask yourself every time you walk out of a social encounter. Did I pick up on someone's worry? Why am I so sensitive to a certain subject? Have I done my best with what I know? Is there something in my past that affects me during specific topics? Remember, it can be easy to take on someone else's feelings if we are already sensitive or passionate about a specific subject.

Questions for Reflection:

1. In your journal, start a mood diary to track 21 days to see how you respond on low-spoons or low-energy days. Are you able to honestly monitor your empathy and respectfully say no more often on these days, either energetically or verbally?
2. What does a low-energy day feel like vs a high-energy day?

3. What can you do to conserve spoons on a low-energy day?

15. Don't Try To Play Therapist

"We ask why she didn't leave instead of how he made her stay. And then we wonder what makes men's violence against women persist to this day."

–Farida D.

Someone once told me, "Dear Best Friend, thank you for being my unpaid therapist." The emotional labor and time one sets aside for their friends is often honorable. The therapist friend feels there is no need for transaction or reciprocation; they just want their friend to be happy and healthy. So what if you stay up until three in the morning every night, holding your friend's hand through the phone and talking them off the phone. This may have felt fulfilling or like it made a difference the first five times, but after the tenth, or twentieth time, you may find your threshold for playing therapist has a limit.

Empaths get sucked into being a discount therapist really easily. Pradhuman Singh Rajpu pointed out that, "The Therapist Friend actually needs the most therapy!" If the therapist's friend has no one to talk to, it is likely that they will keep their troubles and worries about their friends inside, and that will not do them any good.

Good friends tell their friends to see a professional. Therapists have been studying the brain for a long time, and this book might be the most you have ever learned about therapy, for a fraction of the cost.

Therapists are not just there to be a good listener. Therapists are there to treat a number of mental illnesses and ailments of the brain. They are able to guide and navigate their clients through grief, anxiety, trauma, depression, addiction, work stress, and relationships.

Bias and Being Objective

The dynamic between a therapist and a client is not the same as how friendships work. It is the job of a therapist to focus on the needs of the client, keep good boundaries, and help clients reach their goals, but this does not mean they automatically agree with the client on everything. Good friends want their friends to be happy, and will sometimes automatically side with the choices of the person who needs therapy, even if they are wrong.

What works for you, may not work for your friend or partner. I had a partner once tell me that sex would help with anxiety and stress relief. This partner was not only being a terrible therapist, but was manipulating information about the brain and sex's effect on the psyche to suit his desires.

When you know a friend's parents, or past actions, or think very highly of said friend, you are not likely to follow the same dialogue and questioning choices as a therapist. You are going to empathetically feel for their hurt moreso, because they are often someone you have known for a long time.

It is important to be the neutral party sometimes and to just listen. You want to commiserate with them. You want to call that person who hurt your friend, or you want to throw out a rude name to make the friend feel better. You may tell your friend what you think they want to hear in order for them to feel better.

Knowing Your Advice has Consequences

Sometimes we think being a friend means going, "Girl, why don't you just leave him?" which might seem helpful at the time, but leaving an abusive or toxic relationship is a lot more complex than simply leaving. People need help realizing their worth, that they can start over, and to also be able to perceive the behavior from their partner that they are enduring as unacceptable.

213

Friends often give advice based on their own experiences, which therapists are advised and trained not to do. What works for one person may not work for another.

Relationships

It is especially difficult for partners who are born male to seek therapy, due to the expectations of masculinity and how they handle mental stress or depression. One dear empath friend of mine, Jade, had dealt with several male partners over her lifetime that chose to lean on their partner for emotional dumping and mental navigation, rather than consulting a professional. This also leads to that learned helplessness discussed in its respective chapter.

There is a difference between being a supportive partner and being a therapist. A supportive partner does not need to be the recipient of emotional turmoil or the responsible party for helping their partner navigate coping. If the empath partner has the emotional bandwidth, they most certainly can be a sounding board, a shoulder to cry on, or even another person to just coexist with. The energy exchange behind coping skills and problem solving can be a lot if it becomes a daily practice.

Knowing Your Advice has Consequences

Sometimes we think being a friend means going, "Girl, why don't you just leave him?" which might seem helpful at the time, but leaving an abusive or toxic relationship is a lot more complex than simply leaving. People need help realizing their worth, that they can start over, and to also be able to perceive the behavior from their partner that they are enduring as unacceptable.

Friends often give advice based on their own experiences, which therapists are advised and trained not to do. What works for one person may not work for another.

How to Set Boundaries with Friends and Still be a Good Listener

Getting someone the help they need is more important than feeling the high of being helpful or wanted. This can lead to codependency or a vicious cycle of behavior.

A therapist can base their judgment on timing, getting to know the client, and figuring out the right time to divulge a hard truth to the patient.

Ask your friends to consider. "I had a bad day, and I don't think I'm in the right mental place to help with this right now. Can we talk tomorrow?"(Sabatello).

Educate yourself and your friends to be respectful of the goings-on in your respective lives. If one of you just had a miscarriage, you would not want the other to talk about the baby moving around, or your annoying pregnancy symptoms. Many people who have had multiple miscarriages would trade anything to experience morning sickness and lived through the minor bodily annoyances to experience a full pregnancy.

A good way to respond to a friend in crisis is to say, "Do you want advice, a distraction, or just someone to listen?" A friend who was going through a divorce was trying to process the shock of what was happening. They need to express the shock and change that they are experiencing. Since the divorce was already happening, there was not necessarily anything to advise on. This transformed when their divorce was finalized, and co-parenting became a subject that was challenging. This was when advice became very useful because there are more moments without easy answers. Many months later, the divorced friend still gets mad and sad at seemingly random times, when it is likely a trigger that reminds them of the divorce or moments when the relationship was in decline. Often, these difficult emotions may need a distraction. A distraction can be a new project, a joke, or a change in topic.

How Can You Suggest Professional Therapy To Your Friends?

Therapy is preventative care. It's scary when I see a coffee mug that says "Friends, cheaper than therapy." Therapy can be expensive, but landing yourself in the hospital from a heart attack is even more expensive.

Normalize talking about mental health to your friends. Do not tell them, "You need a therapist," or "You should go to therapy." Talk about your therapist. Talk about how your therapist has a therapist. Most, if not all people in mental health counseling have a therapist as well, as it can be quite exhausting and take a toll on even a healthy brain to hear the strife, grief, and tragedy all day long.

A mentor of mine used a metaphor about wearing prescription glasses to see better. If you have trouble seeing, you find out the needs of your eyes, and the right prescription for you allows the world to be seen better. When you see a psychiatrist, therapist, or psychologist, you are given tools to handle and perceive your world better, just like you would with glasses.

Try to get your friends to not treat mental health as secondary to physical health. Anything your body and brain do that gets in the way of your life deserves medical attention. It would be ridiculous to believe that you can think yourself out of strep throat or to just give enough time for it to go away. You would not want to do this with depression either. Even if you give your body or brain time on its own to go away, you may get behind on life and then get more stressed, sending yourself back into a depressive spiral. It also creates stress in your life if you think you do not have time to heal. Trudging through an illness or mental illness can last forever. Learning coping skills, going to therapy, and rerouting your thoughts are all ways to make the mental healing process more expedited, just like how antibiotics would lead to healing from strep throat faster.

There are more complicated processes going on in your brain than in any other part of your body. Trauma, genetic issues, neurodivergence, grief, and general problem solving all deserve attention and opportunities for healing. All the things that impact your body also impact your brain. Having clean water, a home or shelter, good nutrition, and a regular sleep routine all affect the brain and body. Once you realize that all your body systems, including the brain, intermingle with each other on a holistic basis, you cannot really separate the two, can you?

How you see the world and how you feel is just like how your heart shows symptoms. A brain shows symptoms with feelings, actions, and ways of thinking or perceiving the world. The heart shows palpitations, arrhythmia, and tension. We also know from placebo studies that the brain is powerful enough to create physical responses to things if it perceives a threat or change in the body, even if it is not there.

Questions for reflection:

1. What limits and boundaries can you set for your friends, but also maintain being a good listener?
2. Even if you feel your advice is good, do you think there is a problem with your advice being treated as medically accurate? Have you considered its level of usefulness?
3. Consider whether or not guiding someone through an issue if it is usual or unusual. Are you always playing therapist? Or is it only on a rare occasion?

Conclusion

Dark empaths, energy vampires, and narcissists are, as it turns out, not very rare. They may be aware of their actions or may be unaware. They might be malicious, annoying, naive, draining, or exhausting. They are often incapable of their own self-actualization, self-care, and self-reflection, and prefer feeling in control over growth. What is not important is saving them or changing their ways. What is best is so that you are armed with the tools in order to live your best life and protect yourself. The less you can enmesh your energy with theirs, the better.

We only have so many precious years on this planet, in this human life. Now is the time to give yourself the best chance to live your life to the fullest. We do this partially by having meaningful connections, fair boundaries, healthy practices, and an understanding of the self. We can learn to identify toxic people and behaviors and protect ourselves from them so that their energy does not enmesh with ours. If you feel that this book has gotten you closer to your best self, I would love a review of your thoughts.

What you have learned in this book can be life-changing, but it is important to use it. Ten percent of learning is obtaining information, and 90% is putting it into practice and applying it to life in order to make the knowledge stick around and be useful. Your future self will thank you once the process has become a habit.

You have hopefully now understood how to identify narcissists, energy vampires, and dark empaths. You have learned how to protect yourself from folks who would drain your energy and to set proper boundaries and communicate well. By now, you have also gained self-care practices and strategies to create shields or different versions of protection. Additionally, you now have love languages and communication techniques to improve your relationships with people you care about.

Do not despair if you need to pick this book up again. Sometimes people fall out of their habits and need to be reminded. No one is perfect, and it's fine to relearn how to keep healthy boundaries and not reach empathic burnout.

This book is an interpretation of knowledge from psychology, metaphysics, philosophy, real-life experiences, and neuroscience. It is not meant to be a replacement for professional therapy or life-saving forms of medicine for physical and mental health.

It is also not a forever-condemning sin if you were an energy vampire, a dark empath, or a narcissist in the past. If you are choosing to change now, you are ready to become a better version of yourself. That's why you chose this book and chose to read it and have now all the tools and knowledge that you need to implement this change. You can use the references at the end of this book for even further learning.

I am fully grateful for sharing this journey together and hope that you will experience that gratitude as well.

You have now reached the end of this resource for empaths and people trying to find their way. Only 10% of people who pick up this book will complete it, and this tells us a lot about commitment and willpower. People are not able to finish what they started anymore; they may lack focus and dedication, or it just may not be the right time. You read this far though- and that's something that'll get you very far.

Now if you kept on reading until the end of this book, you probably found what you discovered inside useful and valuable. This makes me incredibly happy because this is the reason I wrote this book.

Before you go, I'd love your help with a super quick and easy favor.

Ninety-one percent of readers read comments before they buy, you probably did as well before choosing this book. Honest reviews are vital for young authors like me and help separate helpful books from others.

So if you feel that that book was useful to you and would like to help a fellow friend in making the right choice, I'd be eternally grateful if you could take 10 seconds of your time to give me your opinion. I read all of them. They're an incomparable source of feedback and motivation since I write books to help people and reading that it helps, makes me feel like the months it took me to research and write this book were well worth it.

If you are on audible, hit the three dots in the top right of your device, and click "Rate & Review". Then leave a few sentences about the book with a star rating.

If you are reading on Kindle or an e-reader - you can scroll to the bottom of the book, then swipe up, and it will automatically prompt a review.

If for some reason they have changed either functionality - you can go to the book page on Amazon (or wherever you purchased this) and leave a review right on the page.

Thank you a million times now, and a million times more later. I wish you love, light, peace, and prosperity in your future journey.

References

Adler, L. (2021, June 4). *Martyr Complex and Covert Narcissism: All You Need to Know.* Toxic Ties. Retrieved April 14, 2022, from https://toxicties.com/martyr-complex-covert-narcissism/

Armstrong, K. (2017, December 29). *'I Feel Your Pain': The Neuroscience of Empathy.* Association for Psychological Science - APS. Retrieved April 14, 2022, from https://www.psychologicalscience.org/observer/neuroscience-empathy

Barrett, L. F. (2017). *How Emotions Are Made: The Secret Life of the Brain* (1st ed.). Mariner Books.

Baughman, H. M., Dearing, S., Giammarco, E., & Vernon, P. A. (2012). Relationships between bullying behaviours and the Dark Triad: A study with adults. *Personality and Individual Differences, 52*(5), 571–575. https://doi.org/10.1016/j.paid.2011.11.020

Brummelman, E., Thomaes, S., Nelemans, S. A., Orobio De Castro, B., Overbeek, G., & Bushman, B. J. (2015). Origins of narcissism in children. Proceedings of the National Academy of Sciences, 112(12), 3659–3662. https://doi.org/10.1073/pnas.1420870112

Croft, C. (2021, February 4). *What are the four Control Dramas?* Chris Croft Training. Retrieved February 28, 2022, from https://www.chriscroft.co.uk/what-are-control-dramas/

Derisz, R. (2022, March 29). *What Is a Dark Empath Energy Vampire and How Can You Avoid Them?* Goalcast. Retrieved April 14, 2022, from https://www.goalcast.com/dark-empath-personality-traits-avoid/

Dunbar's number: Why we can only maintain 150 relationships. (n.d.). BBC Future. Retrieved April 14, 2022, from https://www.bbc.com/future/article/20191001-dunbars-number-why-we-can-only-maintain-150-relationships

Esquith, R. (2007). *Teach Like Your Hair's on Fire : The Methods and Madness Inside Room 56* (2007th ed.). Rafe Esquith.

Fisher, R. (2020, October 1). *The surprising downsides of empathy*. BBC Future. Retrieved April 14, 2022, from https://www.bbc.com/future/article/20200930-can-empathy-be-bad-for-you

Fitzpatrick SJ, Kerridge IH, Jordens CFC, Zoloth L, Tollefsen C, Tsomo KL, Jensen MP, Sachedina A, Sarma D. Religious perspectives on human suffering: Implications for medicine and bioethics. Journal of Religion and Health 2016; 55:159–173.

Gillette, H. (2022, February 9). *How to Spot a Dark Empath*. Psych Central. Retrieved February 13, 2022, from https://psychcentral.com/health/what-is-a-dark-empath

Ding, W., Shao, Y., Sun, B., Xie, R., Li, W., & Wang, X. (2018). How Can Prosocial Behavior

Be Motivated? The Different Roles of Moral Judgment, Moral Elevation, and Moral Identity Among the Young Chinese. Frontiers in Psychology, 9. https://doi.org/10.3389/fpsyg.2018.00814

Heym, N., Firth, J., Kibowski, F., Sumich, A., Egan, V., & Bloxsom, C. A. J. (2019). Empathy at the Heart of Darkness: Empathy Deficits That Bind the Dark Triad and Those That Mediate Indirect Relational Aggression. *Frontiers in Psychiatry, 10.* https://doi.org/10.3389/fpsyt.2019.00095

Heym, N., Kibowski, F., Bloxsom, C. A., Blanchard, A., Harper, A., Wallace, L., Firth, J., & Sumich, A. (2021). The Dark Empath: Characterizing dark traits in the presence of empathy. *Personality and Individual Differences, 169*. https://doi.org/10.1016/j.paid.2020.110172

Jaffe, E. (2007, May 1). *Mirror Neurons: How We Reflect on Behavior*. Association for Psychological Science - APS. Retrieved April 14, 2022, from https://www.psychologicalscience.org/observer/mirror-neurons-how-we-reflect-on-behavior

James, A. (2019, December 3). 15 Ways to Stop Energy Vampires Draining Your Life Source. Pocket Mindfulness. Retrieved April 14, 2022, from https://www.pocketmindfulness.com/energy-vampires/

Keen, S. (2006). A Theory of Narrative Empathy. *Narrative 14*(3), 207-236. doi:10.1353/nar.2006.0015.

Gillette, H. (2022, February 9). How to Spot a Dark Empath. Psych Central. Retrieved April 14, 2022, from https://psychcentral.com/health/what-is-a-dark-empath#vs-narcissistic-personality

McLaren, K. (2013). *The Art of Empathy* [E-book]. Sounds True.

Lorelie, C. (2020, August 6). Friend Vs Therapist: Who To Choose & When. Wellnite. Retrieved April 14, 2022, from https://www.wellnite.com/post/pros-cons-therapy-friend

Miserandino, C.*The Spoon Theory* (2013, April 26). But You Dont Look Sick? Retrieved February 13, 2022, from https://butyoudontlooksick.com/articles/written-by-christine/the-spoon-theory/ narcissism | Definition, Origins, Pathology, Behavior, Traits, & Facts. (n.d.). Encyclopedia Britannica.

Retrieved April 18, 2022, from
https://www.britannica.com/science/narcissism

Neo, P. (2021, June 25). *Dark Empaths: The Personality Type That Uses Empathy As A Weapon*. Mbg Relationships. Retrieved April 14, 2022, from
https://www.mindbodygreen.com/articles/what-are-dark-empaths

NHS website. (2021, November 24). Overview - Cognitive behavioural therapy (CBT). NHS. Retrieved April 15, 2022, from
https://www.nhs.uk/mental-health/talking-therapies-medicine-treatments/talking-therapies-and-counselling/cognitive-behavioural-therapy-cbt/overview/ Orloff, J. (2018, April 14). *Are You Drained by an Energy Vampire? Take Dr. Orloff's Quiz*. Judith Orloff MD. Retrieved April 14, 2022, from
https://drjudithorloff.com/quizzes/are-you-drained-by-an-energy-vampire/

Orloff, J. (2021, November 1). *The New Science of Empathy and Empaths*. Judith Orloff MD. Retrieved February 13, 2022, from
https://drjudithorloff.com/the-new-science-of-empathy-and-empaths/

Peric, M. (2022, February 14). Energy Vampires: Things To Learn Before They Suck You Dry. Life Hacks. Retrieved April 15, 2022, from https://lifehacks.io/energy-vampires/

Psych2Go. (2021, January 21). *5 Signs of a Dark Empath - The Most Dangerous Personality Type* [Video]. YouTube.
https://www.youtube.com/watch?v=Tl20Ke2Y58g&ab_channel=Psych2Go

Redfield, J. (1994). *The Celestine Prophecy*. Adfo Books.
Simon, S. (2022, February 7). *Is It Love, or Love Bombing?* verywellhealth. Retrieved April 14, 2022, from
https://www.verywellhealth.com/love-bombing-5217952

Shariatmadari, D. (2020, September 25). *"I'm extremely controversial": the psychologist rethinking human emotion*. The Guardian. Retrieved April 14, 2022, from https://www.theguardian.com/books/2020/sep/25/im-extremely-controversial-the-psychologist-rethinking-human-emotion

Showfety, S. (2022, January 26). *How to Spot a "Dark Empath."* Lifehacker. Retrieved April 14, 2022, from https://lifehacker.com/how-to-spot-a-dark-empath-1848378629

Sabatello, J. (2021, August 2). No, Your Friends Can't Be Your Therapist, HealthyPlace. Retrieved on 2022, April 14 from https://www.healthyplace.com/blogs/relationshipsandmentalillness/2021/8/no-your-friends-cant-be-your-therapist

Spiegel, A. (2017, June 1). *Emotions*. Invisibilia NPR. Retrieved April 14, 2022, from https://www.npr.org/2017/06/01/530928414/emotions-part-one

Stokes, V. (2021, April 6). *Intuitive Empaths: Signs, Types, Downsides, and Self-Care*. Healthline. Retrieved April 14, 2022, from https://www.healthline.com/health/intuitive-empaths

van Dongen, J. D. M. (2020). The Empathic Brain of Psychopaths: From Social Science to Neuroscience in Empathy. Frontiers in Psychology, 11. https://doi.org/10.3389/fpsyg.2020.00695

Zaki, J. (2013, November 7). *Using empathy to use people: Emotional intelligence and manipulation*. Scientific American Blog Network. Retrieved April 14, 2022, from https://blogs.scientificamerican.com/moral-universe/using-empathy-to-use-people-emotional-intelligence-and-manipulation/

Made in United States
Troutdale, OR
08/06/2023

11859244R00128